HIGH SCHOOL SCIENCE

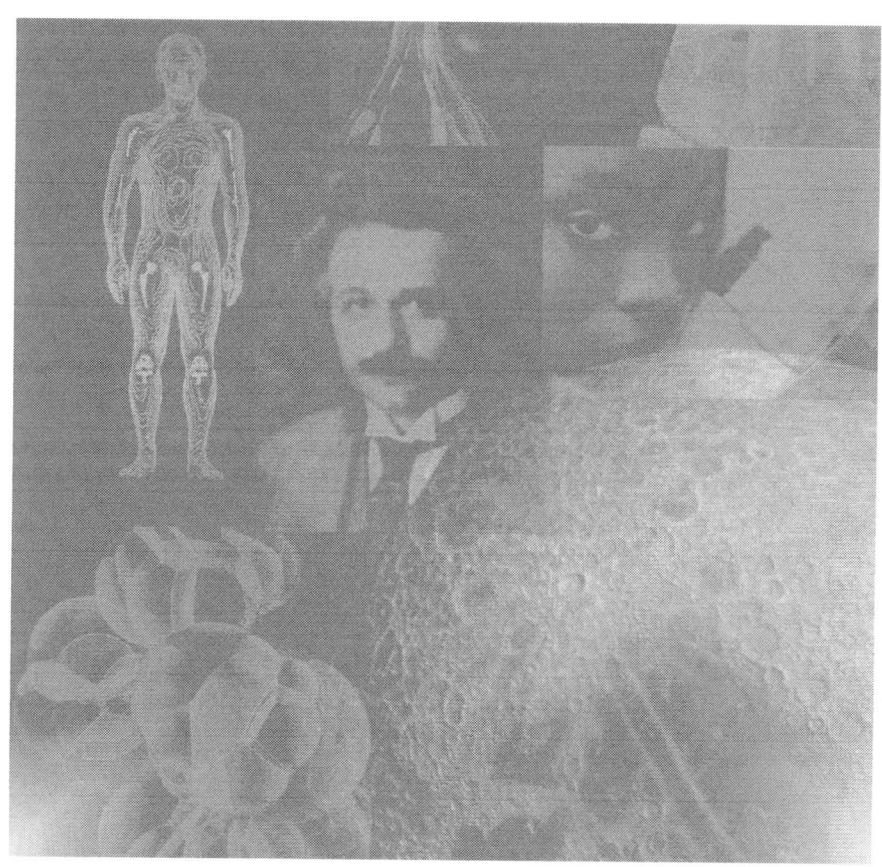

by Jeanne Piscitello
Edited by Sarah M. Williams
Artwork by Brian Espano

Item Code: QWK 4224 • Copyright © 2006 Queue, Inc.

All rights reserved. No part of the material protected by this copyright may be reproduced or utilized in any form or by any means, electronic or mechanical, including photocopying, recording, or by any information storage and retrieval system. Printed in the United States of America.

Queue, Inc. • P.O. Box 156 Fairfield, CT 06824
(800) 232-2224 • Fax: (800) 775-2729 • www.qworkbooks.com

Table of Contents

LIFE SCIENCES: **The Structure of Living Things, Genetics, Evolution, Diversity of Living Things, and the Environment**

Multiple-Choice Questions..1
Open-Ended Questions 29

PHYSICAL SCIENCES: **Matter, Force, and Motion and Energy**

Multiple-Choice Questions..59
Open-Ended Questions 80

EARTH SCIENCES: **Geological Systems, the Universe, and the Environment**

Multiple-Choice Questions..115
Open-Ended Questions 135

Life Sciences
The Structure of Living Things, Genetics, Evolution, Diversity of Living Things, and the Environment

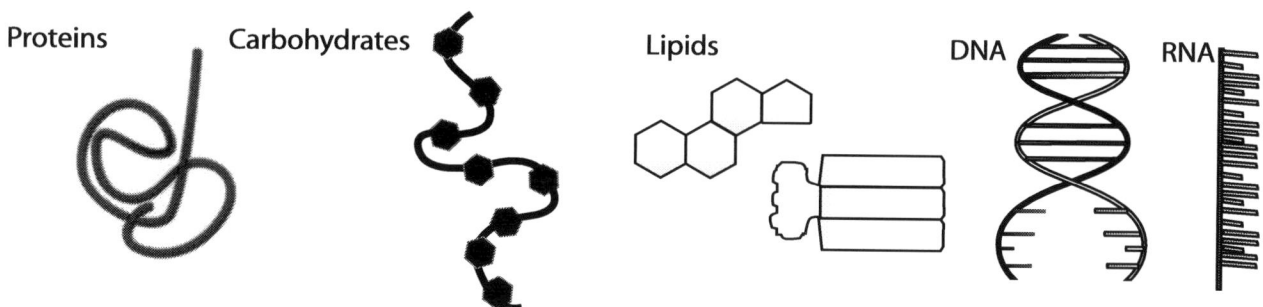

1. Proteins are composed of long chains of smaller subunit molecules called

   A. nucleotides.
   B. amino acids.
   C. simple sugars.
   D. fatty acids.

2. Sucrase is a protein that accelerates the breakdown of sucrose (table sugar) into two smaller sugars. *Sucrase* is an example of what type of protein?

   A. a receptor protein
   B. a structural protein
   C. an enzyme
   D. a transport protein

3. Collagen is a protein found in large amounts in cartilage, a strong and flexible substance found in the skeletal systems of many animals. *Collagen* is an example of a(n)

   A. receptor protein.
   B. structural protein.
   C. enzyme.
   D. transport protein.

4. What two types of molecules in cells are used to supply and store energy?

   A. lipids and proteins
   B. proteins and nucleic acids
   C. carbohydrates and lipids
   D. carbohydrates and proteins

5. Nucleic acids, such as DNA and RNA, are long chains of smaller subunit molecules called

   A. fatty acids.
   B. nucleotides.
   C. monosaccharides.
   D. peptides.

6. The process that provides cells with usable chemical energy involves the conversion of

   A. ATP to ADP.
   B. ADP to ATP.
   C. sugar to starch.
   D. DNA to RNA.

7. Starch and glycogen are carbohydrates found in plant and animal cells, respectively. They are both composed of long chains of glucose. What statement **best** describes these molecules?

   A. Starch and glycogen can be broken down into simpler sugars.
   B. Starch and glycogen most likely serve as sources of stored energy in plant and animal cells.
   C. Starch and glycogen are complex carbohydrates.
   D. all of the above

8. Lipids are a class of molecules found in cells. Lipids have many functions and include fats, oils, and steroids. They differ from the other types of molecules found in cells in that

   A. they are polar molecules and are soluble in water.
   B. they are non-polar molecules and are insoluble in water.
   C. they do not contain carbon.
   D. none of the above.

9. Which of the following statements about DNA and RNA is **not** correct?

   A. Both DNA and RNA are made of nucleotides.
   B. Both DNA and RNA are involved in protein synthesis.
   C. Both DNA and RNA are double-stranded molecules composed of complementary nitrogen base pairs.
   D. Both DNA and RNA are found in the nucleus.

10. DNA contains the information needed to

    A. direct all the activities of a cell.
    B. produce proteins.
    C. produce RNA.
    D. all of the above.

11. All of the following are found in nucleotides **except** a
    A. sugar.
    B. phosphate group.
    C. glycoprotein.
    D. nitrogenous base.

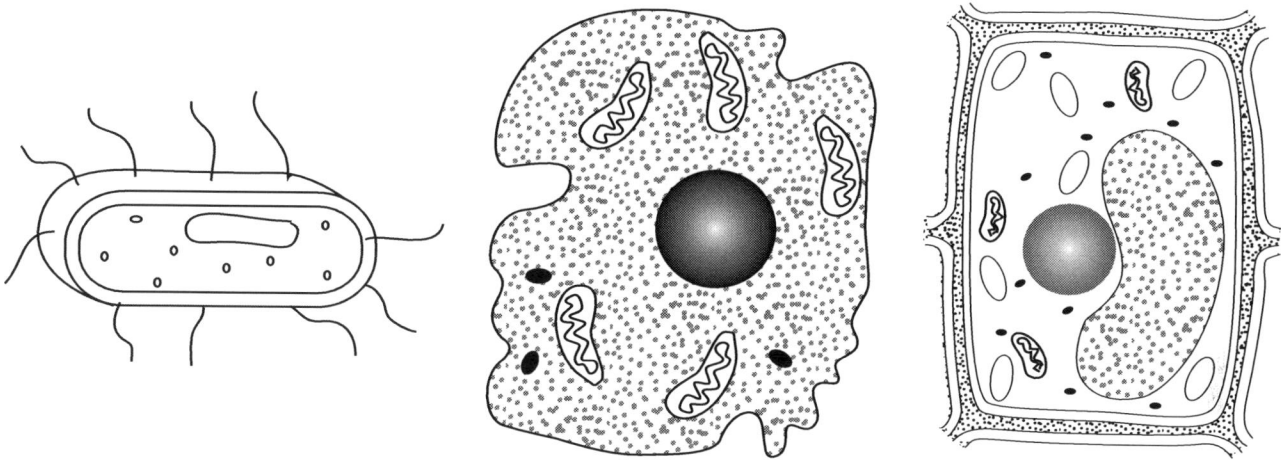

12. There are two different types of cells: prokaryotic cells and eukaryotic cells. How do prokaryotic cells differ from eukaryotic cells?
    A. Prokaryotic cells do not have a cell membrane.
    B. Prokaryotic cells do not contain DNA.
    C. Prokaryotic cells are more advanced cells and are usually found in multicellular organisms.
    D. Prokaryotic cells do not contain membrane-bound organelles.

13. When examining cells under a microscope, what structures indicate that the cells are plant cells?
    A. chloroplasts and mitochondria
    B. a cell wall and a cell membrane
    C. a cell wall and chloroplasts
    D. chloroplasts and vacuoles

14. In animal cells, genetic material is found in which organelle(s)?
    A. in the nucleus and the ribosomes
    B. in the nucleus and the mitochondria
    C. in the nucleus and the chloroplasts
    D. only in the nucleus

15. Which of the following represents the transfer of information in a cell?

   A. DNA to RNA to protein
   B. RNA to DNA to protein
   C. DNA to protein to RNA
   D. DNA to protein to ATP

For questions 16–25, match the cell organelle listed in Column A with its function in Column B.

Column A

____ 16. Cell wall

____ 17. Cell membrane

____ 18. Lysosomes

____ 19. Endoplasmic

____ 20. Chloroplasts

____ 21. Mitochondria

____ 22. Nucleus

____ 23. Ribosomes

____ 24. Cytoplasm

____ 25. Vacuoles

Column B

A. contains the genetic information and the information needed to direct all the cell's activities

B. membrane-bound sacs that digest food particles and worn-out cell structures

C. produces most of the chemical energy used by the cell to fuel the cell's chemical reactions

D. a lipid bilayer that encloses the contents of a cell and reticulum; controls the passage of materials into and out of the cell

E. the space between the nucleus and the cell membrane that contains water, proteins, and cell organelles

F. membrane bound sacs used to store water, nutrients, and wastes

G. site of photosynthesis

H. a network of membranes used to process and transport substances throughout the cell

I. a rigid layer of non-living material that surrounds, supports, and protects cells in plants and some other organisms

J. site of protein synthesis

26. Panceatic cells are involved in the production and secretion of the protein insulin. What organelles would be plentiful in these cells?

    A. ribosomes and mitochondria
    B. vacuoles and lysosomes
    C. ribosomes and endoplasmic reticulum
    D. vacuoles and ribosomes

27. Muscle cells are required to produce tremendous amounts of energy for movement. What organelle(s) would be plentiful in these cells?

    A. ribosomes and mitochondria
    B. mitochondria
    C. chloroplasts and mitochondria
    D. chloroplasts

The following equation represents an important biochemical process in cells. Use this equation to answer questions 28–31.

$$C_6H_{12}O_6 + 6O_2 \longrightarrow 6CO_2 + 6H_2O + ATP$$

glucose + oxygen (yields) carbon dioxide + water + energy

28. What cellular process is represented by this equation?

    A. photosynthesis
    B. cellular respiration
    C. digestion
    D. metabolism

29. The products of this chemical reaction are _____ and _____.

30. The substrates of this chemical reaction are _____ and _____.

31. What molecule supplies the chemical energy that becomes incorporated into ATP?

    A. water
    B. oxygen
    C. glucose
    D. carbon dioxide

32. Most of the important molecules found in cells contain the elements carbon and hydrogen. What two types of molecules found in cells also contain the element nitrogen?

   A. lipids and proteins
   B. carbohydrates and lipids
   C. proteins and carbohydrates
   D. proteins and nucleic acids

33. The process of cellular respiration occurs in three stages and involves the action of many enzymes. The first stage of the process, called *gycolysis*, involves the

   A. partial breakdown of glucose outside the cell.
   B. partial breakdown of glucose in the cytoplasm.
   C. breakdown of glucose in stages in the mitochondria.
   D. breakdown of large food particles in the cytoplasm.

34. The final two stages of cellular respiration provide a cell with most of its chemical energy. Where do these stages of respiration occur?

   A. in chloroplasts in plant cells and mitochondria in animal cells
   B. in mitochondria in both plant and animal cells
   C. in cytoplasm in plant cells and mitochondria in animal cells
   D. none of the above

35. How are the processes of photosynthesis and cellular respiration related?

   A. The end products of photosynthesis become the raw materials of cellular respiration.
   B. The end products of cellular respiration become the raw materials of photosynthesis.
   C. both A and B
   D. none of the above

36. The process of photosynthesis involves the conversion of

   A. energy from sunlight into chemical bond energy in ATP.
   B. energy from ATP into chemical bond energy in sugar.
   C. both A and B.
   D. neither A nor B.

37. Which of the following statements about photosynthesis is true?

    A. Photosynthesis provides our atmosphere with oxygen.
    B. Photosynthesis traps energy from sunlight into molecules that become the source of energy for all living things.
    C. Photosynthesis allows plant cells to make the glucose that is then used in cellular respiration.
    D. all of the above

38. What will happen to the volume of a cell placed in a fluid that has a greater concentration of solutes than the cell?

    A. The volume of the cell will decrease.
    B. The volume of the cell will increase.
    C. The volume of the cell will stay the same.
    D. Not enough information is given.

39. The cell membrane is *semipermeable*. This means that

    A. all materials can pass through the cell membrane freely.
    B. only certain materials—such as water, oxygen, and carbon dioxide—can pass through the cell membrane by simple diffusion.
    C. all materials need to be transported across the cell membrane by mechanisms that require energy.
    D. only water can pass through the cell membrane.

40. How would a cell such as a white blood cell ingest a bacterial cell?

    A. The bacterial cell would diffuse across the cell membrane.
    B. The bacterial cell would be carried across the cell membrane by transport proteins embedded in the cell membrane.
    C. The cell membrane would form a sac around the bacterial cell that would eventually pinch off inside the cell.
    D. Cells cannot ingest other cells.

41. The active transport of materials across a cell membrane involves the expenditure of energy by the cell. Which of the following is an example of active transport?

    A. diffusion of O_2 across a cell membrane
    B. movement of materials through pores in the cell membrane
    C. osmosis
    D. the transport of a molecule across a cell membrane by a transport protein that requires ATP

42. The process of cellular respiration involves the transfer of chemical bond energy from

    A. complex carbohydrates to glucose.
    B. glucose to ATP.
    C. ATP to ADP.
    D. glucose to carbon dioxide and water.

43. The plant pigment that traps energy from sunlight during the process of photosynthesis is

    A. chloroplastin.
    B. chlorophyll.
    C. glucose.
    D. cellulose.

44. During strenuous exercise, cells may not receive enough oxygen to break down sugar and produce the ATP needed by the cell. These cells may start to break down sugar through a chemical process that does not require oxygen. This process is called *anaerobic respiration*. Which of these statements about anaerobic respiration is true?

    A. Anaerobic respiration produces as much energy for the cell as aerobic respiration (respiration in the presence of oxygen).
    B. Anaerobic respiration produces more energy for the cell than aerobic respiration.
    C. Anaerobic respiration produces less energy for the cell than aerobic respiration.
    D. none of the above

45. Many substances move through the cytoplasm of a cell by simple diffusion. During diffusion, these substances move

    A. from an area of greater concentration to an area of lesser concentration.
    B. from an area of lesser concentration to an area of greater concentration.
    C. toward the cell membrane and out of the cell.
    D. randomly through the cytoplasm.

46. What feature do plant cells and bacterial cells **not** have in common?

    A. DNA
    B. cell walls
    C. specialized structures called flagella that help the cell move
    D. genetic material that is contained in a nucleus

47. Some single-celled organisms, called Archaea, live in extreme environments—environments with very high temperatures, high salt concentrations, or very acidic conditions. These organisms are

   A. harmful to the environment.
   B. thought to be closely related to Earth's first life forms.
   C. relatively new forms of life on Earth.
   D. chemically similar to bacteria.

48. Which of the following organisms have prokaryotic cells?

   A. algae
   B. all microorganisms
   C. fungi
   D. bacteria

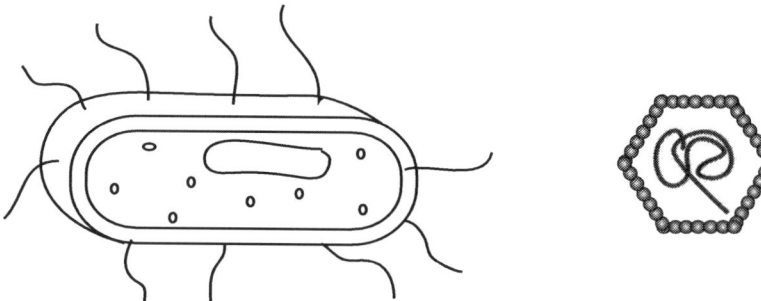

49. What characteristic(s) do viruses have in common with bacteria?

   A. They grow and develop.
   B. They use energy.
   C. They reproduce.
   D. all of the above

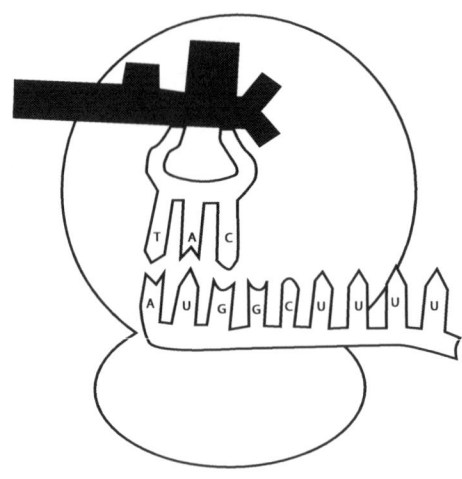

Protein synthesis involves many steps and many molecules. In questions 50–55, match the term in Column A with the term from Column B that best describes its role in protein synthesis.

Column A

____ 50. messenger RNA

____ 51. transfer RNA

____ 52. adenine, thymine, guanine, and cytosine

____ 53. DNA

____ 54. amino acids

____ 55. adenine, uracil, guanine, and cytosine

Column B

A. a group of molecules that become linked chemically to form a protein

B. part of the genome that contains the nucleotide base pair sequence that determines (codes for) the sequence of amino acids in proteins

C. nitrogen bases found in RNA

D. carries the DNA code for protein synthesis from the nucleus to the ribosomes

E. nitrogen bases found in DNA

F. carries the amino acids to the ribosomes

56. Put the four steps of cell division below in order.

____ The cell replicates its DNA.

____ The cell splits into two daughter cells.

____ The cell undergoes mitosis.

____ The cell grows to a critical size.

57. The first step in DNA replication involves the

   A. production of messenger RNA.
   B. unzipping of the two complementary strands of the DNA molecule.
   C. condensing of the DNA molecule into compact structures called chromosomes.
   D. lining up of chromosomes at the center of the cell.

58. Which statement **best** describes the process of DNA replication?

   A. A new molecule of DNA is made using the old molecule as a template.
   B. Two molecules of DNA are made, each using one strand of the original DNA molecule as a template.
   C. Messenger RNA is synthesized and used as a template to make a copy of the DNA.
   D. The DNA molecule breaks apart and is reassembled randomly into two new molecules of DNA.

59. The section of DNA that contains the information for a trait that is passed on from parent to offspring is called a

   A. chromosome.
   B. centriole.
   C. centromere.
   D. gene.

60. The order of the nucleotide base pairs along the length of a DNA molecule determines

   A. the structure and function of individual cells.
   B. the order of amino acids in proteins.
   C. an organism's physical and chemical characteristics.
   D. all of the above.

61. Specific combinations of three nucleotide bases in DNA code for

   A. different types of nucleic acids.
   B. specific amino acids found in proteins.
   C. the structures of carbohydrates.
   D. none of the above.

62. Multicellular organisms are composed of many cells. The DNA in each cell contains

   A. the information that determines the structure and function of that cell.
   B. the information needed for all cells in the organism to function.
   C. the information needed to reproduce the entire organism.
   D. all of the above.

63. Prior to cell division, the DNA molecule replicates and condenses to form visible structures called *chromosomes*. Each chromosome contains

   A. two copies of a section of the parent cell's DNA called sister chromatids.
   B. a single copy of a section of the cell's DNA.
   C. DNA and RNA complexes that the daughter cells will need to produce proteins.
   D. complete copies of the parents cell's genetic material.

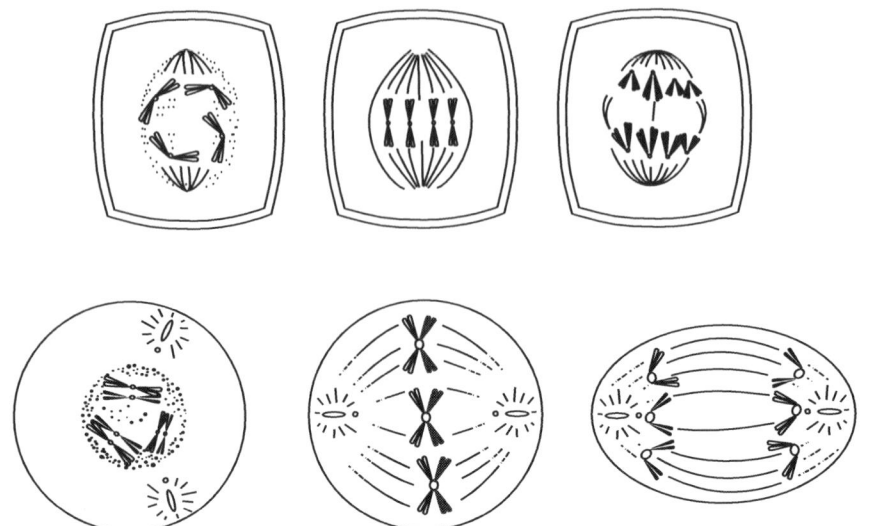

64. During mitosis, the cell

   A. makes copies of its genetic material in preparation for cell division.
   B. distributes copies of its genetic material to opposite ends of the cell.
   C. splits, forming two daughter cells.
   D. nearly doubles in size.

65. When a simple unicellular organism divides, the daughter cells receive

   A. a complete copy of the genome of the parent cell.
   B. half of the genome of the parent cell.
   C. two complete copies of the genome of the parent cell.
   D. none of the above.

66. When an organism produces sex cells, these cells contain _____ the amount of DNA as the parent cell.

   A. the same
   B. half
   C. one quarter
   D. double

67. When DNA replicates, mistakes occur. These mistakes are called *mutations*. In an organism that reproduces sexually,

   A. only the mutations that occur during meiosis are passed on to offspring.
   B. only the mutations that occur during mitosis are passed on to the offspring.
   C. both A and B.
   D. neither A nor B.

68. When a somatic cell in your body like a skin cell divides, it undergoes

   A. meiosis.
   B. mitosis.
   C. both A and B.
   D. none of the above.

*For questions 69–77, determine whether the characteristics apply to the processes of mitosis (**MT**), meiosis (**ME**), or both (**B**) by writing the appropriate letters in the blanks.*

____ 69. two cell divisions occur

____ 70. chromosomes line up at the center of the cell

____ 71. results in the production of four daughter cells

____ 72. all the genetic material of the parent cell is copied

____ 73. the daughter cells receive the same number of chromosomes as the parent cell

____ 74. homologous pairs of chromosomes line up at the center of the cell

____ 75. results in the production of two daughter cells

____ 76. the daughter cells receive 1/2 the number of chromosomes as the parent cell

____ 77. results in the production of egg and sperm cells

78. Genes on homologous pairs of chromosomes that contain information for the same genetic trait are called

   A. factors.
   B. alleles.
   C. hybrids.
   D. insertions.

Pod color was one of the traits in pea plants that Gregor Mendel studied. He found that some pea plants had green pods (G), while others had yellow pods (g). Use this information and that are found in the Punnett squares below to answer questions 79–86.

Trait: Green Pod (G), Yellow Pods (g)

Parent Generation: GG   x   gg
 (green)   (yellow)

F1 Generation:

	G	G
g	Gg (green)	Gg (green)
g	Gg (green)	Gg (green)

Parents: Gg   x   Gg
 (green)   (green)

F2 Generation:

	G	g
G	GG (green)	Gg (green)
g	Gg (green)	gg (yellow)

79. Which trait for pod color is dominant? _____

80. What percentage of the F1 generation is heterozygous for pod color? _____

81. What percentage of the F2 generation is heterozygous for pod color? _____

82. What percentage of the F2 generation is homozygous recessive for pod color? _____

83. What parental genotypes would result in an F1 generation with equal numbers of plants having green and yellow pods?   _____ and _____

84. Can the genotype of a pea plant with yellow pods be determined without breeding the plant?   _____

85. What kind of alleles would G and g be if the plants in the F1 generation had green and yellow spotted pods? _____

86. Which of the following statements about a pea plant from the F1 generation is true?
    A. The DNA of this plant only contains information for producing green pods.
    B. The DNA of this plant does not contain information for producing yellow pods.
    C. The DNA of this pea plant contains the information for producing green and yellow pods, but the information for producing yellow pods is not expressed.
    D. none of the above

87. Which of the following statements about DNA replication is true?
    A. DNA replication always produces identical copies of DNA.
    B. Errors can occur when DNA is replicated.
    C. Errors that occur during DNA replication are corrected at the next cell division.
    D. Errors that occur during DNA replication are always harmful to the daughter cell that received the altered DNA.

A mutation refers to any change in the sequence of the nucleotide base pairs found in a cell's DNA. For 88–91, match the type of mutation listed in Column A with its definition in Column B.

Column A

____ 88. point mutation

____ 89. deletion

____ 90. insertion

____ 91. cross-over

Column B

A. a change in which one or more base pairs are removed or lost from the DNA molecule

B. a change in which extra base pairs are added somewhere along the length of the DNA molecule

C. a change resulting from the exchange of large sections of chromosomes during meiosis

D. a change in which one nitrogen base is substituted for another along the length of the DNA molecule

92. Mutations occur spontaneously and at low rates in nature. Mutations can

    A. be beneficial to an organism.
    B. be harmful to an organism.
    C. have little effect on an organism.
    D. all of the above.

93. In organisms that reproduce asexually, mutations are

    A. always passed on to the next generation.
    B. sometimes passed on to the next generation.
    C. corrected before the cell divides.
    D. always lethal.

94. In organisms that reproduce sexually, mutations are

    A. passed on to all the offspring.
    B. passed on to some of the offspring.
    C. passed on to the offspring if the mutations are beneficial.
    D. expressed in all of the offspring.

95. For many years, people have used selective breeding to develop plants and animals with desirable traits, such as more disease-resistant crops or cows that produce more milk. The selective breeding practice in which two individuals with identical or similar traits are bred is called

    A. cloning.
    B. inbreeding.
    C. out-crossing.
    D. hybridization.

96. When a very productive honeybee is crossed with a more disease-resistant honeybee, the process is called

    A. inbreeding.
    B. hybridization.
    C. genetic engineering.
    D. none of the above.

97. Some plants are grown from small parts of a parent plant called *cuttings*. This technique is a type of

    A. inbreeding.
    B. recombinant DNA technology.
    C. cloning.
    D. hybridization.

98. Dolly is an example of a cloned sheep. To produce Dolly, scientists removed an egg cell from a mature sheep (Sheep A). They then removed the genetic material (nucleus) from this egg and replaced it with the genetic material from a somatic cell from another mature sheep (Sheep B). The egg cell with the new genetic material was then implanted into the uterus of a third sheep (Sheep C). The sheep that was born was named Dolly. Dolly was the clone of

   A. Sheep A.
   B. Sheep B.
   C. Sheep C.
   D. none of the above.

99. Clones occur in nature in the form of

   A. fraternal twins.
   B. identical twins.
   C. both A and B.
   D. none of the above.

100. Recombinant DNA technology allow scientists to

   A. insert human genes into the DNA of bacteria.
   B. insert human genes into the DNA of human cells to cure certain diseases.
   C. insert genes from bacteria and other organisms into the DNA of plant cells to produce heartier varieties of plants.
   D. all of the above.

101. Which of the following statements about genetically engineered organisms is true?

   A. Genetically engineered bacteria are being used to produce medicines to treat diseases in humans.
   B. Genetically engineered cows are being used to produce human proteins used to treat diseases in humans.
   C. Genetically engineered viruses are being used to treat certain diseases in humans.
   D. All of the above are true.

102. Genetic engineering techniques most closely resemble which of the following types of mutation?

   A. point mutations
   B. single base pair substitutions
   C. insertions
   D. deletions

103. Individual members of the same species

    A. are genetically identical.
    B. vary slightly in their genetic makeup.
    C. are physically identical.
    D. none of the above.

104. A group of similar organisms that can mate and produce fertile offspring is called a

    A. phylum.
    B. genus.
    C. biome.
    D. species.

105. The theory of evolution maintains that

    A. species do not change over time.
    B. species undergo gradual changes over time.
    C. all species eventually become extinct.
    D. all members of a species remain genetically identical over time.

106. Environmental changes can

    A. lead to the extinction of a species.
    B. lead to the evolution of a species.
    C. have no effect on the fate of a species over time.
    D. all of the above.

107. All of the following factors play a role in evolution **except**

    A. overproduction of offspring.
    B. competition for available resources.
    C. acquired behaviors.
    D. natural selection.

108. Natural selection favors the inheritance of genes for traits that

    A. enable an organism to better survive in a particular environment.
    B. enable an organism to better survive any environment.
    C. make the organism bigger and faster.
    D. make the organism more intelligent.

109. Traits that make an individual better adapted to a particular environment are

    A. the result of random mutations.
    B. induced by severe changes in the environment.
    C. acquired by an individual throughout its life and passed on to its offspring.
    D. none of the above.

110. The theory of evolution is supported by many lines of evidence. These include all of the following **except**

   A. the fossil record.
   B. similarities in body structures.
   C. similarities in DNA sequences.
   D. similarities in habitat.

111. The bones in the forelimbs or several animals, including a bat, a bird, and a dog, are arranged in a similar fashion. These are called

   A. analogous structures.
   B. homologous structures.
   C. common structures.
   D. developmental anomalies.

112. Similarities in embryonic development provide evidence that organisms

   A. evolved from a common ancestor.
   B. have some genetic material in common.
   C. both A and B.
   D. neither A nor B.

113. The newest method used to determine evolutionary relationships among species involves

   A. the determination of similarities in DNA sequences and protein structures.
   B. fossil records.
   C. new techniques in dissection.
   D. none of the above.

114. Scientists now think that all life on earth evolved from

   A. a type of bacteria.
   B. a type of green algae.
   C. fungus.
   D. protists.

115. Human beings are most closely related to

   A. dinosaurs.
   B. mammals.
   C. primates.
   D. cephalopods.

116. Which of the following is **not** associated with the formulation of the theory of evolution?

    A. Charles Darwin
    B. the Galapagos Islands
    C. Gregor Mendel
    D. finches and marine iguanas

117. The rapid evolution of new species over short periods of time is called the theory of

    A. gradualism.
    B. punctuated equilibria.
    C. mass extinction.
    D. rapid mutation.

118. If two species have few if any DNA base pair differences in their genes for a certain protein, these species

    A. are most likely closely related.
    B. only distantly related.
    C. are unrelated species.
    D. There is not enough information given to determine evolutionary relationships.

119. The scientific name for the house cat is *Felis domesticus*. Which of the following organisms has the most characteristics in common with the house cat?

    A. *Ursus horribilis*
    B. *Musca domestica*
    C. *Felis concolor*
    D. Not enough information is provided.

120. Biologists use seven levels to classify living things based on their common characteristics. The broadest level of classification is the kingdom, followed by

    A. phylum, order, class, family, genus, and species.
    B. phylum, class, order, family, genus, and species.
    C. order, phylum, family, class, genus, and species.
    D. phylum, class, order, family, species, and genus.

121. Plants and animals are two of six kingdoms of living things. The remaining four kingdoms include all of the following **except**

    A. Bacteria.
    B. Fungus.
    C. Protists.
    D. Chordates.

122. Viruses are

    A. the smallest known living things.
    B. nonliving infectious particles that can only reproduce inside of living cells.
    C. infectious pieces of DNA or RNA.
    D. nonliving infectious particles that reproduce outside of cells.

123. Viruses infect _____ cells.

    A. animal
    B. plant
    C. bacterial
    D. all of the above

124. You would find all of the following in a virus **except**

    A. proteins.
    B. DNA or RNA.
    C. enzymes.
    D. ribosomes.

125. Which of the following cell structures would never be found in a bacterial cell?

    A. a cell wall
    B. a cell membrane
    C. ribosomes
    D. a nucleus

126. Which group of organisms live in extreme environments and are thought to be closely related to earth's first living things?

    A. Bacteriophages
    B. Archaea
    C. Bacteria
    D. Prions

127. Some bacteria form structures called *endospores*. These are small round structures that contain the genetic material and some cytoplasm. Endospores enable bacteria to

    A. exchange genetic material with other bacteria.
    B. undergo sexual reproduction.
    C. survive in harsh environmental conditions for long periods of time.
    D. infect other organisms.

The group of organisms in the Kingdom Protista have many varied characteristics. Some are plant-like, some are animal-like, and some are fungus-like. In questions 128–131, match the protist in Column A with its characteristics in column B.

Column A

____ 128. ameba

____ 129. algae

____ 130. slime molds and mildews

____ 131. paramecium

Column B

A. organisms that cannot make their own food, have cell walls, and reproduce by spores

B. fairly complex microorganisms that cannot make their own food; move by the beating of hair-like projections called cilia

C. organisms that make their own food and provide the world with most of its oxygen

D. organisms that cannot make their own food and use pseudopodia or false feet to move and engulf food particles

132. Fungi are heterotrophs. What structures do they use to digest and absorb nutrients?

   A. a conjugation tube
   B. hyphae
   C. pseudopods
   D. an oral groove

133. What two groups of organisms play an important role as decomposers?

   A. bacteria and fungi
   B. viruses and bacteria
   C. protists and fungi
   D. none of the above

134. Fungi are known to form mutually beneficial relationships with other organisms, including

   A. algae.
   B. autotrophic bacteria.
   C. plants.
   D. all of the above.

135. Terrestrial plants are thought to have evolved from

   A. fungi.
   B. green algae.
   C. bacteria.
   D. lichens.

136. The life cycles of all plants include the production of all of the following **except**

   A. spores.
   B. seeds.
   C. sperm cells.
   D. egg cells.

137. Only some plants have vascular tissue that transports water and nutrients throughout the plant. Which of the following types of plants do **not** have vascular tissue?

   A. gymnosperms
   B. mosses
   C. ferns
   D. angiosperms

138. Which group of plants produces seeds and flowers?

   A. mosses
   B. ferns
   C. gymnosperms
   D. angiosperms

139. Which group of plants produces "naked seeds" that are dispersed mostly by the wind?

   A. mosses
   B. ferns
   C. gymnosperms
   D. angiosperms

140. A major evolutionary advance in seed-producing vascular plants was the enclosure of sperm cells in

   A. the pistil.
   B. pollen grains.
   C. fruit.
   D. seeds.

141. All of the following are reproductive parts of a flower **except** the

    A. stamen.
    B. pistil.
    C. stigma.
    D. sepals.

142. All of the following are parts of a seed **except**

    A. the seed coat.
    B. stored food.
    C. the plant embryo.
    D. a cuticle.

143. Organisms that must obtain food by consuming other organisms include all of the following **except**

    A. heterotrophs.
    B. carnivores.
    C. herbivores.
    D. autotrophs.

144. Multicellular organisms can have several levels of cellular organization. The highest level of cellular organization is represented by which of the following structures?

    A. a specialized cell like a muscle cell
    B. epithelial tissue
    C. the heart
    D. the nervous system

145. Which of the following statements about animals is **not** true?

    A. All animals are multicellular.
    B. All animals are eukaryotic.
    C. All animals have cells organized into tissues, organs, and organ systems.
    D. All animals are heterotrophs.

146. An animal that has only one line of symmetry that divides it into mirror images has

    A. radial symmetry.
    B. bilateral symmetry.
    C. no symmetry.
    D. no distinct front or back ends.

In questions 147–158, match the group of organisms in Column A with the description in Column B.

Column A

___ 147. sponges

___ 148. cnidarians

___ 149. worms

___ 150. mollusks

___ 151. arthropods

___ 152. echinoderms

___ 153. chordates

___ 154. fish

___ 155. amphibians

___ 156. reptiles

___ 157. birds

___ 158. mammals

Column B

A. bilaterally symmetrical invertebrates with soft, unsegmented bodies often covered with hard outer shells

B. radially symmetrical marine invertebrates with spiny skin, internal skeletons, and tube feet

C. bilaterally symmetrical invertebrates with exoskeletons, segmented bodies, and jointed appendages

D. simple asymmetrical invertebrates with no tissues or organs; their bodies can be described as sacs with pores through which water flows

E. radially symmetrical invertebrates that are most noted for being carnivores with stinging cells on tentacles

F. includes three groups of bilaterally symmetrical invertebrates with tissues, organs, and organ systems; many are parasitic and some have segmented bodies

G. these thin-skinned vertebrates are ectothermal and live the first part of their lives in water and much of their adult lives on land; they have jelly-like eggs and always return to the water to reproduce

H. endothermic vertebrates with hollow bones, a highly efficient four-chambered heart, and bodies adapted for flight

I. All organisms in this phylum have a notochord, a dorsal nerve cord, and pharyngeal slits at some point in their lives.

J. endothermic vertebrates with a four-chambered heart, hair or fur, and produce milk to nourish their young

K. ectothermic vertebrates with scaly waterproof skin and other characteristics that allowed them to be the first group of organisms adapted to live their entire lives on land

L. most of these vertebrates are ectothermic, have scales, have fins for movement through water and obtain O_2 through structures called gills

159. Which statement lists the following levels of ecological organization from the simplest to the broadest?

   A. organism, community, population, ecosystem
   B. organism, habitat, community, ecosystem
   C. organism, population, community, ecosystem
   D. organism, habitat, ecosystem, community

Hawks, snakes, prairie grasses, bison, and many other organisms live together in an area called a prairie. This area has certain resources such as amount of available water, sunlight, temperature, and type of soil. Use this information and the following terms to complete statements 160–166.

biome	ecosystem	habitat	nitch
biosphere	abiotic factors	biotic factors	

160. The prairie is an example of a(n) _____.

161. The area within the prairie where the hawk lives and obtains the things it needs, such as food, water, and shelter, is called its _____.

162. The living things found on the prairie, such as the plants, grasses, hawks, and other organisms that interact with each other are referred to as _____.

163. The non-living things found on the prairie, such as the water, sunlight, temperature, and soil, are referred to as _____.

164. A prairie is a type of grassland. Prairies, savannas, and other areas with similar climates and organisms are called a type of _____.

165. All the organisms found on a prairie are part of a higher level of ecological organization called the _____.

166. The snake, hawk, and each type of organism living on the prairie have a particular role in this environment. This role is called their _____.

The following paragraph describes the interactions between a group of living things on the prairie. Use the information in this paragraph to answer questions 167–171.

These are many different types of living things on the prairie. Fungi and bacteria are found in the soil. These organisms help break down dead animal and plant matter and return the nutrients to the soil. These nutrients are taken up by the many types of plants and grasses that use the energy from sunlight to make their own food. Large bison graze on the grass. The seeds and berries made by the plants and grasses provide food for the prairie dogs and other small mammals, such as mice and rats. Hawks, eagles, and badgers hunt the prairie dogs and even larger animals like wolves hunt the bison.

167. Which of the following organisms on the prairie are producers?

　　A. fungi and bacteria
　　B. grasses and plants
　　C. bison
　　D. eagles

168. Which of the following organisms on the prairie are primary consumers?

　　A. bison
　　B. fungi and bacteria
　　C. badgers
　　D. all of the above

169. Which of the following organisms on the prairie are secondary consumers?

　　A. prairie dogs
　　B. hawks
　　C. bison
　　D. plants and grasses

170. Which of the following organisms on the prairie are decomposers?

   A. wolves
   B. eagles
   C. bacteria and fungi
   D. none of the above

171. Which of the organisms describes is at the top of the food chain?

   A. hawks
   B. wolves
   C. badgers
   D. bison

1. When a microscopic particle (particle X) found on a space probe was examined under a microscope, it was thought to resemble a cell. What characteristics would it have to have to be considered a living thing?

2. Describe the basic structure and function of proteins.

3. Describe the basic structure and function of carbohydrates.

4. Describe the basic structure and function of lipids.

5. Describe the basic structure and function of nucleic acids.

6. What role do complex carbohydrates such as starch and glycogen play in providing a cell with energy?

7. How are DNA and RNA similar? How do they differ?

8. How do the processes of photosynthesis and cellular respiration complement each other?

9. How would a mutation that resulted in non-functional mitochondria affect a cell?

10. Describe the structure of DNA and outline the steps in DNA replication.

11. While studying a sample of microscopic organisms, a scientist observed a larger than normal single-celled organism with two nuclei. How might this have occurred?

12. What role does meiosis play in passing on genetic traits from parents to offspring?

13. What is the significance of crossing over?

14. How can a difference in a single base pair along a length of DNA that codes for a particular protein result in a defective protein?

15. Describe how continental drift contributed to the evolution of species on two or more continents.

16. What is the theory of evolution and what lines of evidence led Charles Darwin to formulate this theory?

17. How does the cell membrane control the passage of materials into and out of the cell?

18. What are the basic characteristics of bacteria?

19. Describe the general characteristics of the Protists. Are these microorganisms more advanced than bacteria? How are they related to other eukaryotes?

20. Not all microorganisms are germs. Many are quite helpful. Describe some of the ways microorganisms are beneficial to humans and other organisms.

21. Plants that live on land evolved from those that lived in water. What kinds of adaptations were necessary to make this move possible?

22. Describe how overproduction, competition, variation, adaptation, and natural selection result in the process of evolution.

23. Giraffes are herbivores with very long necks. They graze on grass and on leaves. Describe how overproduction, competition, variation, adaptation, and natural selection may have affected the evolution of the giraffe.

24. What is the relationship between natural selection and gene mutation?

25. Redwood trees are some of the tallest plants on Earth. Why would you expect these trees to have vascular tissue?

26. Compare the characteristics of Gymnosperms and Angiosperms.

27. There are three groups, or phyla, of worms. Their bodies are surprisingly well organized. Describe two of their more advanced features.

28. Compare the processes of complete and incomplete metamorphosis.

29. Compare how different classes of vertebrates obtain oxygen from their environment.

30. What is happening to the Earth's populations of amphibians and what might it mean to other species?

31. *All mammals give birth to live fully developed young.* Explain why this statement is false.

32. Why are amphibians and reptiles rarely found in cold climates, while birds and mammals are?

33. What is AIDS and how is it spread?

34. Describe three causes of species extinction and give examples of each.

35. Describe the relationship between predator and prey populations and how an imbalance in their populations can be harmful to an area.

36. A lichen is an example of two organisms living in a symbiotic relationship. Describe the three types of symbiosis.

37. How is the nitrogen cycle a form of recycling?

Several methods have been used to develop strains of plants or breeds of animals with desirable characteristics. These methods include selective breeding, and the more recent methods of cloning and genetic engineering. In questions 38–40, describe how selective breeding, cloning, and genetic engineering techniques benefit society.

38. Selective Breeding

39. Cloning

40. **Genetic engineering**

41. What is gene therapy and how can it be used to treat disease?

Physical Sciences
Matter, Force, and Motion and Energy

1. Matter is defined as anything that has

   A. weight.
   B. mass.
   C. weight and volume.
   D. mass and volume.

2. The fundamental units of matter, also called the building blocks of matter, are

   A. molecules.
   B. compounds.
   C. atoms.
   D. electrons.

3. Which of the following scientists proposed the atomic theory of matter?

   A. Niels Bohr
   B. John Dalton
   C. Albert Einstein
   D. Ernest Rutherford

4. The central region of an atom, called the *nucleus*,

   A. has a net positive charge.
   B. has a net negative charge.
   C. is electrically neutral.
   D. none of the above.

5. Electrons are

   A. subatomic particles with very little mass.
   B. subatomic particles that are found orbiting the nucleus of an atom.
   C. subatomic particles that are involved in chemical bonding.
   D. all of the above.

6. Atoms that are electrically neutral have no net charge because the number of electrons equals the

    A. number of protons.
    B. total number of particles in the nucleus.
    C. number of neutrons.
    D. atomic mass.

7. A rock sample is found to have two types of carbon atoms. One has an atomic mass of 12 and the other has an atomic mass of 14. The two types of carbon atoms have

    A. different numbers of protons.
    B. different numbers of particles in their nuclei.
    C. different arrangements of electrons around their nuclei.
    D. different chemical properties.

8. Three isotopes of hydrogen have atomic masses of 1, 2 and 3, respectively. These three isotopes have

    A. different chemical properties.
    B. different numbers of neutrons.
    C. different net charges.
    D. different numbers of electrons available for chemical bonding.

9. An element with 7 protons, 7 neutrons, and 7 electrons has an atomic number of

    A. 7.
    B. 14.
    C. 21.
    D. none of the above.

10. Nearly all of the mass of an atom is found

    A. distributed throughout the electron shells.
    B. in the outermost electron shells.
    C. concentrated in the nucleus.
    D. distributed evenly throughout the atom.

11. Which scientist discovered that atoms contained smaller subatomic particles?

    A. Democritus
    B. Niels Bohr
    C. John Dalton
    D. Joseph Thompson

12. Which statement **best** describes the model of the atom proposed by Niels Bohr?

    A. Electrons travel around the nucleus of the atom in fixed paths or orbits.
    B. Electrons are held in fixed positions within the nucleus of the atom.
    C. Electrons circle the nucleus of an atom forming an "electron Cloud."
    D. none of the above

13. According to the electron cloud theory of the atom, electrons are found

    A. traveling in fixed orbits around the nucleus.
    B. traveling freely within shells or energy levels located at certain distances from the nucleus.
    C. at no predictable location within the atom.
    D. none of the above.

14. According to the electron cloud theory, the first and second energy levels or electron shells can accommodate

    A. 1 and 2 electrons, respectively.
    B. 2 electron each.
    C. 2 and 8 electrons, respectively.
    D. 8 electrons each.

15. According to the electron-cloud theory, there are at least seven electron shells or energy levels. The most energetic electrons are found

    A. in the electron shell located closest to the nucleus.
    B. in the electron shell located furthest from the nucleus.
    C. distributed randomly throughout all the energy levels.
    D. distributed in pairs in each energy level.

16. When atoms form chemical bonds, they seek to

    A. complete or fill their outermost electron shell.
    B. remain electrically neutral.
    C. rid themselves of low-energy electrons.
    D. gain or lose protons.

17. Our atmosphere contains the gases hydrogen, nitrogen, and oxygen. Their molecular formulas are H_2, N_2 and O_2, respectively. These substances are examples of

    A. compounds.
    B. elements.
    C. isotopes.
    D. ions.

18. Our atmosphere also contains the gas, carbon dioxide. Its molecular formula is CO_2. Carbon dioxide is an example of a(n)

   A. compound.
   B. element.
   C. atom.
   D. ion.

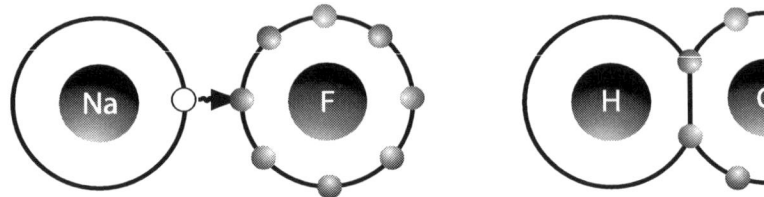

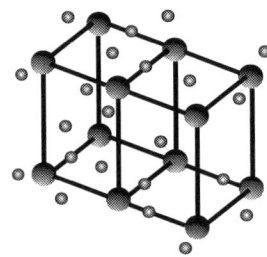

19. What type of bond is formed when each of two atoms share one or more electrons?

   A. a hydrogen bond
   B. an ionic bond
   C. a covalent bond
   D. a metallic bond

20. A sodium atom will transfer one electron to a chlorine atom to form the compound sodium chloride commonly known as table salt. The type of bond found in NaCl is a(n) _____ bond.

   A. non-polar covalent
   B. hydrogen
   C. ionic
   D. polar covalent

21. Ionically-bonded compounds like sodium chloride contain two charged atoms or molecules. These compounds have

    A. a net positive charge.
    B. a net negative charge.
    C. positively and negatively charged ions whose charges are balanced to produce no net charge.
    D. Not enough information is given.

22. When an atom of oxygen forms a double covalent bond with another oxygen atom, the total number of electrons shared is

    A. 2.
    B. 4.
    C. 6.
    D. 8.

23. When oxygen forms two single covalent bonds with two hydrogen atoms to form water (H_2O), the shared electrons

    A. are shared equally between the oxygen and hydrogen atoms.
    B. are shared unequally, being drawn more to the oxygen nucleus.
    C. are shared unequally, giving the water molecule a net negative charge of two.
    D. none of the above.

24. The electrons involved in chemical bonding are

    A. found furthest from the nucleus.
    B. the most energetic electrons.
    C. found in the outermost electron shell.
    D. all of the above.

25. Unequal *sharing* of electrons occurs in

    A. ionic bonds.
    B. polar covalent bonds.
    C. non-polar covalent bands.
    D. only in double and triple covalent bonds.

26. Hydrogen gas has a chemical formula of H_2. The two hydrogen molecules share one pair of electrons. Which of the following represents this molecule?

    A. H-H
    B. H=H
    C. H/H
    D. none of the above

27. In which of the following substances would you find a sea of mobile electrons surrounding several nuclei?

    A. water (H_2O)
    B. carbon dioxide (CO_2)
    C. copper (Cu)
    D. calcium chloride ($CaCl_2$)

28. How many oxygen molecules do the following molecules contain?

    $Pb(NO_3)_2$ $FeSO_4$ $MgCO_3$

    A. 3, 4 and 3
    B. 2, 4 and 3
    C. 6, 4 and 3
    D. 6, 4 and 4

29. The following is an equation for a balanced chemical reaction:

    $MgCO_3 + 2\ HCl \longrightarrow MgCl_2 + H_2O + CO_2$

    The substrates in this reaction include

    A. H_2O.
    B. $MgCl_2$.
    C. $MgCO_3$.
    D. two of the above.

Balance the following chemical equations.

30. ___Au + ___O_2 $\longrightarrow$ ___Au_2O_3

31. ___Na + ___H_2O $\longrightarrow$ ___NaOH + ___H_2

*There are four basic types of chemical reactions: synthesis reactions (**S**), decomposition reactions (**D**), single displacement reactions (**SD**), and double displacement reactions (**DD**). In questions 32–37, identify the type of reaction represented by each equation.*

___ 32. $2Na + Cl_2 \rightarrow 2NaCl$

___ 33. $Zn + 2HCl \rightarrow ZnCl2 + H$

___ 34. $CaCO_3 \rightarrow CaO + CO_2$

___ 35. $Pb(NO_3)_2 + 2KI \rightarrow PbI_2 + 2KNO_3$

___ 36. $Fe + CuSO_4 \rightarrow FeSO_4 + Cu$

___ 37. $2H_2 + O_2 \rightarrow 2H_2O$

38. An explosion of a firecracker is an example of

    A. an endothermic reaction.
    B. a chemical reaction that absorbs heat.
    C. an exothermic reaction.
    D. a reaction that has no activation energy.

39. The following reaction is an endothermic reaction:

    $2NaCl \rightarrow 2Na + Cl_2$

    Which of the following statements about this reaction is true?

    A. The products of this reaction absorb energy.
    B. The products of this reaction lose energy to their surroundings.
    C. This reaction does not involve any net gain or loss of energy.
    D. This reaction is spontaneous.

40. What statement(s) is (are) true of all chemical reactions?

    A. All chemical reactions involve a rearrangement of atoms.
    B. All chemical reactions result in changes in the physical and chemical properties of the reactants.
    C. All chemical reactions involve the breaking of existing chemical bonds and the formation of new chemical bonds.
    D. All of the above are true of chemical reactions.

41. What type of atom will **not** form a chemical bond with another atom?

    A. an atom with an outermost electron shell that is not full
    B. an atom with an outermost electron shell that is full
    C. an atom with less than two valence electrons
    D. an atom that is electrically neutral

42. Some chemical reactions involve

    A. the production of atoms.
    B. the destruction of atoms.
    C. both A or B.
    D. none of the above.

43. Some chemical reactions occur very quickly, others more slowly. The measure of how quickly products are formed in a chemical reaction is called the *rate of the reaction*. Generally speaking, reaction rates increase with all of the following **except**

    A. greater concentrations of reactants.
    B. increasing surface area of the reactants.
    C. greater temperatures.
    D. fewer molecules of reactants per unit volume.

44. Substances called *catalysts* increase the rate of chemical reactions by

    A. increasing the activation energy needed for the reaction.
    B. decreasing the activation energy needed for the reaction.
    C. increasing the rate of molecular collisions between reactants.
    D. increasing the energy involved in the molecular collisions between the reactants.

45. When substances containing the element carbon, such as coal and petroleum products, are burned, what harmful product is released into the environment?

    A. CO_2
    B. CH_4
    C. C_2H_5OH
    D. $C_6H_{12}O_6$

46. The first scientist to arrange the known elements into rows and columns called the Periodic Table of Elements was

    A. Galileo.
    B. Dmitri Mendeleev.
    C. Niels Bohr.
    D. Madame Curie.

47. In the first version of the Periodic Table, elements were arranged into rows and columns in order of increasing

    A. number of electrons.
    B. atomic mass.
    C. diameter of the nucleus.
    D. atomic number.

48. The Periodic Table was later revised because of a significant discovery by Henry Moseley. Moseley's discovery led to a Periodic Table with the elements arranged in order of

    A. increasing atomic mass.
    B. increasing atomic number.
    C. increasing pH.
    D. increasing chemical reactivity.

49. The modern Periodic Table demonstrates that the atomic number of an element determines

    A. its physical properties.
    B. its chemical properties.
    C. its electron configuration.
    D. all of the above.

50. The elements Li, Na, and K belong to the same group (family) in the Periodic Table. Li, Na, and K share all of the following characteristics **except**

    A. similar physical properties.
    B. similar chemical reactivities.
    C. the same number of valence electrons.
    D. the same atomic number.

51. The elements Na, Mg, P, and Cl are found in the same horizontal row (period) in the Periodic Table. Na, Mg, P, and Cl have

    A. similar physical properties.
    B. similar chemical reactivities.
    C. the same number of valence electrons.
    D. different numbers of valence electrons.

For 52–61, match the term in Column A with the description in Column B.

Column A

___ 52. metal

___ 53. period

___ 54. halogens

___ 55. transition metals

___ 56. alkali metals

___ 57. nonmetals

___ 58. family

___ 59. rare-earth metals

___ 60. alkaline earth metals

___ 61. noble gases

Column B

A. members of this group or family have one valence electron and are the most reactive family of metals

B. elements with the same number of valence electrons

C. members of this family have two valence electrons and are the second most active group of metals

D. a family of unreactive elements with complete outermost electron shells

E. elements with increasing atomic numbers from left to right

F. the most reactive family of nonmetals whose members need one electron to complete their outermost electron shell

G. several families of elements that include copper, tin, iron, silver, and gold, whose properties differ from those of the other metals

H. elements that are shiny, are good conductors of electricity and heat, and are ductile and malleable

I. elements that have no luster, are poor conductors of heat and electricity, and are neither malleable nor ductile

J. a group of metals that include radioactive elements

62. Which of the following scientists was associated with the discovery of radium and polonium?

   A. Albert Einstein
   B. Marie Curie
   C. Ernest Rutherford
   D. John Dalton

63. What type of force keeps the electrons orbiting the nucleus?

   A. the electromagnetic force of attraction
   B. a force within the atom called the weak force
   C. the electromagnetic force of repulsion
   D. the force of gravity

64. What two opposing forces act on the protons and keep them contained in the nucleus?

   A. the electromagnetic force of attraction and the strong force
   B. the electromagnetic force of repulsion and the strong force
   C. the strong force and the weak force
   D. the electromagnetic force of repulsion and the weak force

65. The strongest force within the atom is

   A. the electromagnetic forces of repulsion and attraction.
   B. the strong force.
   C. the weak force.
   D. gravity.

66. The weakest and least understood force within the atom is

   A. the electromagnetic forces of repulsion and attraction.
   B. the strong force.
   C. the weak force.
   D. gravity.

67. The weak force is responsible for

   A. the conversion of a neutron into a proton and an electron.
   B. radioactive decay.
   C. both A and B.
   D. none of the above.

68. Radioactive elements include all of the following **except**

   A. certain isotopes of C.
   B. uranium.
   C. all elements that produce fluorescence.
   D. the two isotopes of H, deuterium and tritium.

*For questions 69–72, indicate which of the following characteristics is associated with alpha particles (**A**) and/or beta particles (**B**).*

____ 69. a particle containing two protons and two neutrons

____ 70. an electron formed inside a nucleus when a neutron breaks apart

____ 71. the weakest type of nuclear radiation

____ 72. the most penetrating type of particle radiation

73. Radioactive elements are those elements that have an unstable nucleus. Which of the following statements describes an unstable nucleus?

    A. An unstable nucleus has more neutrons than protons.
    B. An unstable nucleus needs less energy to break it apart than a stable nucleus.
    C. An unstable nucleus does not undergo nuclear reactions.
    D. all of the above

74. Gamma rays are a type of nuclear radiation. They are also a type of electromagnetic wave. How do gamma rays differ from other types of electromagnetic waves, such as ultraviolet radiation?

    A. Ultraviolet rays are given off by the sun; gamma rays are not.
    B. Gamma rays have a higher frequency, shorter wavelength, and more energy than ultraviolet rays.
    C. Gamma rays are visible; ultraviolet rays are not.
    D. Gamma rays are damaging to living things; ultraviolet rays are not.

For questions 75–80, match the term in column A with the best description in column B.

Column A

___ 75. alpha decay

___ 76. nuclear fission

___ 77. nuclear chain reaction

___ 78. beta decay

___ 79. nuclear fusion

___ 80. gamma decay

Column B

A. type of nuclear decay that produces a new atom with an atomic number greater than the original by one

B. type of nuclear decay that results in an atom with a nucleus with a lower energy state

C. process whereby two atomic nuclei are joined to form one nucleus with a greater mass

D. process whereby an atomic nucleus is split into two smaller nuclei with similar atomic masses

E. a continuous series of nuclear fission reactions that releases huge amounts of energy

F. type of nuclear decay that produces a new atom with an atomic mass decreased by four and an atomic number decreased by two

81. The conversion of hydrogen into helium at the core of the sun is an example of

   A. nuclear fission.
   B. alpha decay.
   C. beta decay.
   D. nuclear fusion.

82. Nuclear fission chain-reactions release tremendous amounts of energy. This energy results from

   A. the release of heat.
   B. the conversion of mass into energy each time one of many nuclei are split.
   C. radioactive decay.
   D. none of the above.

83. Enrico Fermi was the first physicist to bombard atomic nuclei with

    A. protons.
    B. neutrons.
    C. alpha particles.
    D. other nuclei.

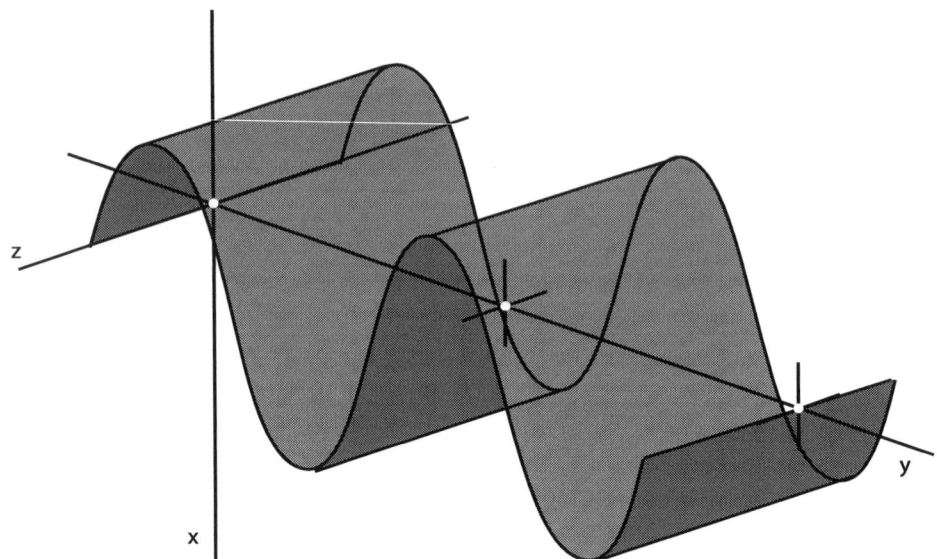

84. Like all waves, electromagnetic waves are characterized by their

    A. amplitude.
    B. wavelength.
    C. frequency.
    D. all of the above.

85. Which of the following statements about electromagnetic waves is **not** true?

    A. All electromagnetic waves travel at speeds greater than the speed of light.
    B. All electromagnetic waves result from vibrating electric and magnetic fields.
    C. All electromagnetic waves can travel through a vacuum.
    D. The source of all electromagnetic waves is a charge that is changing speed or direction.

86. The electromagnetic spectrum refers to the range of electromagnetic radiations emitted by the sun. Which of the following pairs includes a type of wave that is **not** part of the electromagnetic spectrum?

    A. ultraviolet light and infrared rays
    B. X-rays and gamma rays
    C. radio waves and microwaves
    D. sound waves and radio waves

87. The amount of energy associated with an electromagnetic wave increases with

   A. increasing wavelength.
   B. decreasing wavelength.
   C. increasing charge.
   D. none of the above.

88. Since all electromagnetic waves travel at the same speed and speed is the product of frequency and wavelength, how are the frequency and wavelength of an electromagnetic wave related?

   A. As the frequency increases, the wavelength increases.
   B. As the frequency decreases, the wavelength increases.
   C. The frequency varies directly with the wavelength.
   D. none of the above

89. There is a force that extends outward through space from charged particles such as protons and electrons. This force is called

   A. an electric field.
   B. gravity.
   C. a current.
   D. magnetism.

90. A neutral object

   A. contains atoms with equal numbers of protons and electrons.
   B. contains atoms with equal numbers of positive and negative charges.
   C. can become charged when its atoms gain or lose electrons.
   D. all of the above.

91. The buildup of an electric charges on an object is called

   A. an electric current.
   B. an electric field.
   C. static electricity.
   D. an electric discharge.

92. Which statement **best** describes an electric potential difference?

   A. the movement of electrons through a wire
   B. the amount of work needed to move a charge between two points
   C. the buildup of electrons on a neutral object
   D. the pull of gravity on an electric charge

93. Which statement **best** describes an electric current?

    A. the amount of charge that passes a given point in a conductor in a given time
    B. the amount of work needed to move a charge between two points in a conductor
    C. the gain or loss of electrons by a neutral object
    D. the pull of gravity on an electric charge

94. Which statement about an electric potential difference is false?

    A. An electric potential difference can be positive.
    B. An electric potential difference can be negative.
    C. An electric potential difference can be neutral.
    D. An electric potential difference is measured in volts.

95. Which of the following devices do the work needed to move electric charges?

    A. batteries
    B. photocells
    C. thermocouples
    D. all of the above

96. Individual atoms have magnetic fields. These fields are the result of the

    A. movement of the atom.
    B. movement of the electrons within the atom.
    C. movement of the atom's nucleus.
    D. attraction between the charged particles in the atom.

97. Magnetism is a force of attraction or repulsion of a magnetic material for certain other materials. This force is produced by

    A. the alignment of the magnetic fields of groups of atoms in the material.
    B. the random arrangement of the magnetic fields of groups of atoms in the material.
    C. the combined force of the electric fields surrounding the charged particles in the atoms in the materials.
    D. none of the above.

98. What will happen to a compass if it is placed near a wire carrying an electric current?

    A. The compass needle will point North.
    B. The compass needle will point South.
    C. The compass needle will align itself with the wire.
    D. The compass needle will spin continually.

99. Which scientist discovered that an electric current produces a magnetic field?

    A. Benjamin Franklin
    B. Hans Christian Oersted
    C. William Gilbert
    D. Charles Ohm

100. What happens to the electrons in a conductor like a coil of copper wire when a magnet is moved back and forth through the center of the wire coil?

    A. The behavior of the electrons in the wire is unchanged.
    B. The electrons orbit the nuclei faster.
    C. The electrons flow through the wire, creating an electric current.
    D. The electrons lose their charge.

101. What statement(s) is (are) true about the relationship between a magnetic field and an electric current?

    A. An electric current is produced in a conductor when a magnet is moved past a conductor.
    B. An electric current is produced in a conductor when the conductor is moved through a stationary magnetic field.
    C. A changing magnetic field will produce an electric current in a conductor.
    D. All of the above are true.

102. The phenomenon of electromagnetic induction is most associated with

    A. Michael Faraday.
    B. Joseph Henry.
    C. Benjamin Franklin.
    D. Andre Ampere.

103. Electromagnetism is used to

    A. produce electricity in simple electrical generator.
    B. produce large amounts of electricity in major power plants.
    C. produce strong electromagnets used in industry.
    D. all of the above.

104. Which of the following does **not** involve mechanical energy?

    A. a wave hitting the shore
    B. sound
    C. a windmill
    D. a burning log

105. How does heat energy affect the behavior of atoms?

    A. Heat causes atoms to move more slowly.
    B. Heat causes atoms to move closer to each other.
    C. Heat causes atoms to move faster.
    D. Heat decreases the attractions between atoms.

106. When bonds between atoms are broken, energy is released. This energy is called *chemical bond energy*. Which of the following examples involves the release of chemical bond energy?

    A. the burning of fuel in a rocket
    B. the digestion of food
    C. an explosion
    D. all of the above

The energy of motion is called kinetic energy. The following equation is used to calculate the kinetic energy of an object:

$$\text{Kinetic Energy} = (\text{mass} \times \text{velocity}^2)/2$$

107. Which of the following objects has the most kinetic energy?

    A. a 8,000 lb vehicle traveling at 5 miles/hr
    B. a 4,000 lb vehicle traveling at 10 miles/hr
    C. a 2,000 lb vehicle traveling at 5 miles/hr
    D. a 2,000 lb vehicle traveling at 10 miles/hr

108. Which two vehicles in question 107 have the same amount of kinetic energy?

    A. A and C
    B. A and D
    C. A and B
    D. All the vehicles in question 107 have different amounts of kinetic energy.

109. What would most increase the kinetic energy of a 2000 lb vehicle traveling at five miles per hour?

    A. Add 2,000 lb of cargo to the vehicle.
    B. Increase its speed to 10 miles/hr.
    C. Add 4,000 lb of cargo to the vehicle.
    D. Add 8,000 lb of cargo to the vehicle.

110. A truck is losing speed as it travels up a hill. At what location will the truck have a maximum potential energy?

   A. at the top of the hill
   B. halfway up the hill
   C. halfway down the hill
   D. at the bottom of the hill

111. All of the following are examples of objects with potential energy **except** a

   A. wound-up spring in a watch.
   B. 12 lb bowling ball at rest in the gutter.
   C. candy bar.
   D. lump of coal.

112. The strength of the gravitation force of attraction between two masses is

   A. proportional to the total mass and the distance between the masses.
   B. proportional to the total mass and inversely proportional to the square of the distance between the masses.
   C. directly proportional to the total mass and inversely proportional to the distance between the masses.
   D. proportional to the total mass, but unrelated to the distance between the masses.

113. The moon has a smaller mass then the Earth. Its gravitational pull on objects is

   A. greater than that of the Earth.
   B. less than that of the Earth.
   C. the same as that of the Earth.
   D. the moon has no force of gravity.

114. Weightless objects in space experience no gravitational pull because they

   A. have no mass.
   B. are traveling too fast to be affected by a gravitational field.
   C. are too far from the sun to be affected by its force of gravity.
   D. are too far from any large mass to be affected by its force of gravity.

115. Objects with relatively little mass

   A. exert no gravitational pull on other masses.
   B. exert relatively small forces of gravitational attraction on other masses.
   C. can have very strong forces of gravity depending on their density.
   D. none of the above.

116. Which condition would result in the greatest increase in the gravitational force of attraction between the Sun and the Earth?

   A. if the mass of the Sun doubled
   B. if the mass of the Earth doubled
   C. if the distance between the Sun and the Earth halved
   D. if the distance between the Sun and the Earth doubled

117. Which pair of objects will repel each other?

   A. two clouds with excess negative charges
   B. two negatively charged ions
   C. two electrons in the same energy level of an atom
   D. all of the above

118. Which pair of objects will attract each other?

   A. two electrons in different energy levels of an atom
   B. two oppositely charged ions, such as Na+ and Cl-
   C. two ions with different negative charges
   D. two objects that have lost electrons

119. The strength of the force of attraction or repulsion between charged objects is

   A. proportional to the charges and the distance between them.
   B. proportional to the charges and inversely proportional to the square of the distance between the charged objects.
   C. proportional to the charges and inversely proportional to the distance between the charged objects.
   D. proportional to the charges, but unrelated to the distance between the charged objects.

120. Which of the following is **not** an example of static electricity?

   A. an excess of electric charges on a rug
   B. the build up of electrons on a cloud
   C. an object that has lost several electrons
   D. the movement of electric charges through water

*Newton developed three Laws of Motion. Which of the terms or conditions described in questions 121–130 are examples of or most associated with Newton's first (**1**), second (**2**), or third (**3**) laws of motion?*

_____ 121. a satellite traveling with a constant velocity through space

_____ 122. a man pushing against a door that will not open

_____ 123. force = mass x acceleration

_____ 124. the Law of Inertia

_____ 125. a fastball hit into left field

_____ 126. For every action, there is an equal an opposite reaction.

_____ 127. A car stops suddenly and the driver lunges forward.

_____ 128. A truck gains more speed traveling downhill than the small sedan in front of it.

_____ 129. Large SUVs have poor gas mileage.

_____ 130. a rocket engine propelling a rocket off the launch pad

131. An object thrown into the air will eventually slow down and come to a complete stop. This is due to

   A. the force of gravity.
   B. the force of friction.
   C. both A and B.
   D. none of the above.

132. Newton's Third Law of Motion is about

   A. the relationship between force and acceleration.
   B. unbalanced forces.
   C. equal and opposite forces.
   D. the force needed to put an object into motion.

1. Define mass, weight, volume, and density in terms of atoms and subatomic particles.

2. Describe how the mass and weight of an object differ on Earth, on the moon, and in space.

3. How would you determine the mass, volume, and density of an irregularly shaped moon rock about the size of a walnut?

4. Describe the atomic theory proposed by John Dalton in 1803.

5. How does J.J. Thomson's model of the atom differ from Ernest Rutherford's model and the model of the atom proposed by Niels Bohr?

6. Describe the basis of the electron cloud theory of the atom.

7. Scientists found two types of carbon atoms in a rock sample. One type of atom had an atomic number of 6, an atomic mass of 14, and no charge (Atom X). The other type of atom also had an atomic number of 6 and no charge, but its atomic mass was 12 (Atom Y). What does this information tell you about the structure of these atoms?

8. Where would you expect to find the electrons in an atom with an atomic number of 10? Refer to the electron cloud theory in your answer.

9. What does the electron configuration of the atom in question 5 tell us about its reactivity?

10. How do the chemical bonds in a covalently bonded molecule like H_2O and a ionically bonded molecule like NaCl differ?

11. Give examples of compounds with covalent and ionic bonds.

12. The single covalent bonds in water are polar covalent bonds. What are polar covalent bonds and how do they affect the properties of the water molecule?

13. Nails are formed from molten iron. Nails made of iron can rust after exposure to water and air. Which of these changes is the result of a chemical reaction? Explain your answers.

14. How does a synthesis reaction differ from a decomposition reaction? Use balanced chemical equations as examples.

15. How does a single-displacement reaction differ from a double-displacement reaction? Use balanced chemical equations as examples.

16. Balance the following equations.

    A. ___Al_2O_3 → ___AL + ___O_2

    B. ___CO_2 + ___H_2O → $C_6H_{12}O_6$ + ___O_2

    C. $C_{12}H_{22}O_{11}$ → ___C + ___H_2O

    D. ___LiBr + ___$Pb(NO_3)$ → ___$LiNO_3$ + $PbBr_2$

17. A meteorite lands in a field near your home. You rush to the field and see an object emitting a faint glow. Is the object radioactive? Is it safe to approach or touch the object? Why or why not?

18. Since its discovery, radioactivity has been put to many uses. Describe some of the ways society benefits from the use of radioactive materials.

19. Objects that are moving have momentum. What is momentum? Describe a home run in terms of momentum.

For questions 20–22, describe Newton's three Laws of Motion and describe a situation that illustrates each of these laws.

20. **First Law of Motion**

21. **Second Law of Motion**

22. **Third Law of Motion**

23. List the four ways a force can affect the movement of an object. Give an example of each.

24. A group of auto engineers want to test the effectiveness of a newly designed seat belt. They decide to use three different types of vehicles in their test—a small sedan (Vehicle 1), a compact SUV (Vehicle II), and a large SUV (Vehicle III). Each vehicle is accelerated down a quarter-mile test track at the end of which is a cement wall. A crash test dummy is strapped into the driver's seat of each vehicle. Use the data in the table below to determine the force with which each vehicle will hit the cement wall.

	Mass	Initial Velocity	Final Velocity	Initial Time	Final Time
Vehicle I	750 kg	0 m/s	3.6 km/s	0 s	10 s
Vehicle II	1,600 kg	0 m/s	4.8 km/s	0 s	12 s
Vehicle III	2,400 kg	0 m/s	6.0 km/s	0 s	15 s

25. Describe the force of friction and instances in which friction is helpful.

26. Describe four forms of energy and give examples of each.

27. Explain what happens to the molecules in an ice cube as the ice is heated to over 100 degrees Celcius.

28. Describe the movement of a child on a swing in terms of potential and kinetic energy.

29. What is an energy conversion and how does the law of conservation of energy apply to energy conversions? Give examples in your answer.

30. What is the relationship between matter and energy in terms of matter-energy conversions?

31. What is static electricity and why does it pull some objects but push others?

32. What is lightning?

33. You are kicking a soccer ball around in an open field when a storm approaches very suddenly. A downpour is accompanied by both lightning and thunder. What should you do to protect yourself from a lightning strike?

34. It is very dry outside on the playground. Susan takes her wool hat off and her hair follows it. Why is Susan having a bad hair day?

35. What is an electric current and how is one produced?

36. Describe the relationship between electric current, resistance and superconductors.

37. Describe parts of an electric circuit found in your home.

38. What is the relationship between electricity and magnetism?

39. What is an electromagnet?

40. Describe the flow of energy in a power plant that uses nuclear fusion to generate electricity.

41. What are the advantages (benefits) and disadvantages (costs) to the use of nuclear reactors to generate electricity?

42. Two people are fishing in a rowboat that is at rest on a calm lake. A motorboat speeds past them, creating waves in the water. Describe the movement of their rowboat in terms of the amplitude, wavelength, and frequency of the wave created by the speeding boat.

43. Your friend thinks that sound waves are the same as radio waves. Is he correct? Explain your answer.

44. How does society benefit from the use of the sonar, radar, and lasers?

45. Consumers can install active or passive solar heating systems in their homes. Both types of systems enable the homeowner to use the energy from the sun to help heat their homes. How do these systems operate?

46. What is the photoelectric effect and how has it changed our thinking about the nature of light?

Earth Sciences
Geological Systems, the Universe, and the Environment

1. Weather is the state of the atmosphere in a specific time and place. The good description of the weather in any given place includes all of the following **except**

   A. the amount and type of clouds.
   B. temperature.
   C. latitude and longitude.
   D. wind speed and direction.

2. A storm with 45–50 mile-per-hour winds is approaching. You check the Beaufort Scale to determine

   A. the probable direction of the winds.
   B. the extent of damage to expect from the winds.
   C. changes in air pressure associated with the storm.
   D. the speed at which the storm is traveling.

3. While flying in an airplane at an altitude of about ten kilometers above the earth's surface, you would

   A. be much too low to observe weather events.
   B. be much too high to be observe weather events.
   C. be at an altitude where you could be flying through a cloud or observing lightning around you.
   D. none of the above.

4. Air is a mixture of gases. Its main components are

   A. nitrogen and oxygen.
   B. nitrogen and carbon dioxide.
   C. oxygen and carbon dioxide.
   D. oxygen and water vapor.

5. The amount of which of the following components of air varies the greatest?

   A. nitrogen
   B. carbon dioxide
   C. oxygen
   D. water vapor

6. Your family lives along the Gulf coast and is preparing for a hurricane. Hurricanes are

   A. storms with high winds and heavy rains that form over warm tropical waters.
   B. storms that lessen in intensity as they move onto land.
   C. storms that create extensive damage, especially where they make landfall.
   D. all of the above.

7. The most damage associated with hurricanes is usually the result of

   A. high winds.
   B. heavy rains.
   C. strong storm surges.
   D. lightning strikes.

8. Your grandparents live in New England. They want to move to the southern Atlantic coast to avoid the snowy winters, but they are concerned about hurricanes. What is the **best** place you could recommend that they build their new home?

   A. several miles inland along a river that leads to the Atlantic Ocean
   B. along the coastline
   C. along the coastline, but in an area sheltered by many trees
   D. several miles inland in a non-flood zone

9. There are many cities in the United States that are located along major rivers. These rivers sometimes overflow their banks and cause major flooding. All of the following factors can contribute to this flooding **except**

   A. prolonged periods of heavy rainfall.
   B. late winter or early spring thaws.
   C. drought conditions.
   D. large drainage basins, which fill the river with extensive amounts of runoff.

10. How do unusually warm temperatures in winter and early spring lead to river flooding?

    A. The snow in the higher elevations does not fully melt.
    B. The runoff from the rapidly melting snow increases because the ground is still frozen and cannot absorb the water.
    C. Mudslides contribute to the flooding.
    D. none of the above

11. A small town is located at the base of the valley of a small mountain stream. One day, there is a particularly heavy downpour. The residents of this town and the surrounding area

   A. are in no danger at all.
   B. may experience severe damage due to flash flooding.
   C. may have some backyard flooding at most.
   D. will have exceptionally good fishing for several days.

12. To prevent flooding in an area, residents should

   A. preserve the natural vegetation.
   B. restore vegetation that has been removed by planting trees, shrubs, and grass.
   C. limit the amount of concrete and asphalt laid down.
   D. all of the above.

13. Communities can **best** protect their homes from flooding by

   A. restricting the commercial use of rivers.
   B. restricting land development in surrounding areas.
   C. filling in lakes, ponds and swamps in the surrounding area.
   D. restricting the building of dams and spillways.

14. Greenhouse gases are thought to be causing changes in weather patterns by

   A. allowing too much of the heat from the sun to escape from our atmosphere.
   B. trapping the heat from the sun in the atmosphere.
   C. depleting the ozone layer and allowing more UV radiation to reach the earth.
   D. creating more acidic precipitation.

15. Greenhouse gases could result in all of the following **except**

   A. global warming.
   B. global cooling.
   C. drought conditions in certain areas.
   D. lower levels of sea water and beach erosion.

16. The burning of fossil fuels, such as coal and oil, releases many gases into the atmosphere. Which of these gases is most responsible for the "greenhouse effect"?

   A. carbon monoxide
   B. carbon dioxide
   C. sulfur dioxide
   D. nitrogen oxide

17. Massive amounts of land in the rainforests have been cleared for farming and raising cattle. As trees are burned to clear the land,

   A. more CO_2 is released into the atmosphere.
   B. less CO_2 is removed from the atmosphere.
   C. less O_2 is released into the atmosphere.
   D. all of the above.

18. Reducing our use of spray cans and refrigerants helps the environment by

   A. reducing the number of greenhouse gases.
   B. preserving the ozone layer.
   C. both A and B.
   D. none of the above.

19. "Acid rain" can take the form of

   A. dry particulates.
   B. rain.
   C. fog.
   D. all of the above.

20. Acid rain is another detrimental effect of burning fossil fuels. Acid rain or acid precipitation is produced

   A. when sulfur dioxide and nitrogen oxides combine with water in the atmosphere to form acids.
   B. when gases and particulates resulting from fossil fuel combustion produce smog.
   C. when carbon dioxide reacts with water in the atmosphere to produce an acid.
   D. only when fossil fuels are burned in nearby areas.

21. A lake in Canada is lifeless and the surrounding forests are being destroyed. The area is sparsely populated. There is no industry and no farming. This situation is most likely the result of

   A. drought conditions brought on by global warming.
   B. eutrophication.
   C. acid rain.
   D. toxic runoff.

22. What might we see if the ozone layer continues to be depleted?

   A. more acid rain
   B. greater incidences of skin cancers
   C. warmer temperatures worldwide
   D. all of the above

23. The ozone molecules that protect us from the harmful effects of UV radiation are

    A. formed from the reaction of chlorofluorocarbons and UV light.
    B. located within a mile of the earth's surface.
    C. found only over the Arctic and the Antarctic.
    D. located 10–15 miles high in the atmosphere.

24. Most of the Earth's fresh water is located in

    A. ice caps and glaciers.
    B. larger bodies of water like lakes.
    C. the ground (groundwater).
    D. rivers and streams.

25. Most of the usable fresh water comes from

    A. melting glaciers.
    B. small streams.
    C. the ground.
    D. large bodies of water like rivers and lakes.

26. Industrial processes produce many toxic byproducts, such as chemicals, lead, and mercury. These materials often end up in streams, rivers, and lakes through

    A. illegal dumping.
    B. runoff from waste disposal sites.
    C. seepage from underground storage containers.
    D. all of the above.

27. The use of chemicals called *phosphates* in laundry detergents is now illegal in many states because phosphates

    A. can cause a lethal overgrowth of algae in lakes and other bodies of water.
    B. are toxic to many types of fish and amphibians.
    C. react chemically with the dissolved O_2 in water.
    D. are harmful to many aquatic plants.

28. Shellfish beds in coastal communities are most often harmed by

    A. acid rain.
    B. overuse of chemical fertilizers.
    C. untreated or poorly treated sewerage.
    D. oil spills.

29. Sources of groundwater pollution include

   A. pesticides.
   B. fertilizers.
   C. used motor oil.
   D. all of the above.

30. In order to limit the pollution of groundwater in residential communities, many towns have banned the use of

   A. above-ground tanks for home heating fuel.
   B. in-ground tanks for home heating fuel.
   C. hot water heaters.
   D. in-ground swimming pools.

31. What would most likely happen to the wildlife in and around a pond contaminated by toxic waste from a nearby factory?

   A. The pond water is depleted of O_2 and the pond inhabitants die.
   B. The toxic material builds up in the fish and other pond inhabitants, eventually killing them and/or the birds and other wildlife that eat them.
   C. Harmful bacteria begin to grow in the pond.
   D. Animals will leave the area and drink from other ponds.

32. Which of the following statements is **not** true about offshore oil spills?

   A. Damage from these oil spills is usually contained within a small area.
   B. The oil can travel to distant beaches and wetlands, harming the inhabitants of these areas as well.
   C. The oil is toxic to many organisms.
   D. The oil is especially harmful to seabirds, coating their feathers and preventing them from swimming and diving to catch fish.

33. Many factories and power plants use water from local waterways to cool equipment. When this heated water is returned to these waterways,

   A. smelly algae grows in the warmer waters.
   B. the warmer water leads to lower levels of O_2 available for the inhabitants of the waterway.
   C. harmful bacteria begin to grow in the warmer water.
   D. all of the above.

34. A small pond surrounded by farmlands experienced eutrophication. This was most likely due to

    A. acid rain.
    B. irrigation of nearby farmlands.
    C. runoff containing chemical fertilizers.
    D. toxic waste from a factory downstream from the pond.

35. Society's attitudes toward pollution are affected by which of the following factors?

    A. individual values
    B. economic considerations
    C. political factors
    D. all of the above

36. Which of the following statements about the process of risk assessment is true?

    A. Risk assessment evaluates only short-term risks.
    B. Determining and evaluating risk is often difficult and imprecise.
    C. Risk assessment is not quantitative.
    D. Risk assessment is well accepted by everyone.

37. Today, experts are advising societies to concentrate on

    A. cleaning up pollution rather than preventing it.
    B. preventing pollution rather than cleaning it up.
    C. continuing economic development at all cost.
    D. preserving our standard of living.

38. An intangible loss cannot be measured in numbers like economic loss. Which of the following is an example of an *intangible loss*?

    A. the depletion of a non-renewable resource
    B. the health effects of a chemical pollutant
    C. the loss of an endangered species
    D. the loss of land used for farming

39. Members of your community are being asked to vote on legislation to limit the use of chemical pesticides and fertilizers by non-commercial property owners. When deciding how to vote, residents will most likely be guided by

    A. the economic impact of the restrictions.
    B. personal values.
    C. considerations of future health issues.
    D. all of the above.

40. Some members of your high school decide to campaign in favor of the restrictions. They are trying to get residents to see themselves as stewards of the environment. Which of the following factors might these students be most concerned about?

   A. detrimental effects of these chemicals on plants, animals, and local habitats
   B. property values
   C. loss of jobs in the community
   D. long-term health risks to property owners

41. Many residents in favor of the restrictions argue that reducing the chemical pollution of the local waterways and groundwater will save money in the long run by

   A. preventing future health problems.
   B. eliminating the need for costly cleanup measures in the future.
   C. both A and B.
   D. neither A nor B.

42. The formation of clay minerals from feldspar is an example of

   A. erosion.
   B. mechanical weathering.
   C. chemical weathering.
   D. deposition.

43. The life processes of both plants and animals, as well as the decay of their remains,

   A. can result in chemical weathering of rocks.
   B. can result in the mechanical weathering of rocks.
   C. both A and B.
   D. Processes of rock weathering are not influenced or aided by biological factors.

44. The deposition of soil and rock by moving water can result in

   A. the wearing down of existing landforms.
   B. the formation of new landforms.
   C. only minimal changes in the surface features of the Earth.
   D. none of the above.

45. Indicate which of the following resources and energy sources are renewable (**R**) and which are non-renewable (**NR**).

   ____ water power

   ____ fossil fuels like petroleum, coal, and natural gas

   ____ atmospheric oxygen and carbon dioxide

   ____ metals, such as iron and copper

   ____ geothermal energy (heat from within the Earth)

   ____ nonmetals like sand, gravel, and building stones

   ____ uranium

   ____ wind

   ____ solar energy

46. The levels of oxygen and carbon dioxide in our atmosphere are renewed by the processes of

   A. photosynthesis and transpiration.
   B. respiration and photosynthesis.
   C. photosynthesis alone.
   D. respiration alone.

47. The amount of land and soil available for farming may be thought of as a renewable resource; however, several human practices can limit their renewablility. These factors include all of the following **except**

   A. use of land for housing and development.
   B. poor farming practices that deplete the soil of nutrients.
   C. practices that allow valuable soil to be removed by wind and rain.
   D. the use of organic fertilizers.

48. The traditional model of the Earth maintains that the Earth consists of four layers: the inner core, the outer core, the mantle, and the crust. If you could travel to the inner core, you would find

   A. a variety of rocks composed mostly of silicon.
   B. a sphere of solid iron and nickel.
   C. flowing liquid rock called magma.
   D. lightweight rocks and soil.

49. What would you find in the Earth's outer core?

    A. a variety of rocks composed mostly of silicon
    B. liquid iron and nickel
    C. a thick layer of heavy rocks
    D. a thin band of lightweight rocks

50. The most recent model of the Earth maintains that

    A. the crust and the uppermost part of the mantle—the layer beneath the crust—form one layer called the lithosphere.
    B. the lithosphere rests on a layer within the mantle called the asthenosphere.
    C. the lithosphere is composed of rigid and moving pieces.
    D. all of the above.

51. The rigid moving pieces that make up the lithosphere are called

    A. continents.
    B. plates.
    C. faults.
    D. abyssal plains.

52. Large areas of less dense rock found on the surface of the denser lithospheric plates are

    A. mountain ranges.
    B. continents.
    C. abyssal plains.
    D. deep-sea trenches.

53. What causes the lithospheric plates to move?

    A. convection currents of partially melted rock (magma) in the asthenosphere
    B. currents of liquid rock in the inner core
    C. disturbances in the outer core
    D. all of the above

In questions 54–61, match the type of movement of the lithospheric plates or geological phenomenon described in Column A with the possible causes in Column B.

Column A

___ 54. lithospheric plates move apart

___ 55. lithospheric plates are pulled together

___ 56. earthquakes form

___ 57. volcanic eruptions occur

___ 58. a fault forms

___ 59. deep-sea trenches form

___ 60. the earth's crust folds and mountain ranges form

___ 61. a mid-ocean ridge forms

Column B

A. stresses cause fractures to form along the boundaries of two plates

B. molten rock moves up to the earth's surface along the boundaries of two plates

C. whenever cooler convection currents within the asthenosphere sink

D. whenever warmer convection currents within the asthenosphere rise

E. whenever two lithospheric plates carrying continents collide, forming a single continent; this is a type of converging boundary called a collision boundary

F. whenever lithospheric plates under water move apart; this is also known as a diverging boundary

G. whenever lithospheric plates slide past each other along their boundaries, causing a crack in the Earth's crust

H. whenever two lithospheric plates converge with one plate plunging under or beneath the other; this is a type of converging boundary known as a subduction boundary

62. The earthquakes that originate deepest in the Earth occur at _____ boundaries.
   A. collision
   B. subduction
   C. diverging
   D. none of the above

63. Geologists use several lines of evidence to determine the changes that took place in the Earth over millions of years. These lines of evidence include

    A. topographical features of the Earth.
    B. radiometric dating.
    C. rock stratification.
    D. all of the above.

64. The geological timetable of the major events that occurred on our planet over time is divided into eras, periods, and epochs based on

    A. the formation of certain rocks.
    B. fossil records.
    C. both A and B.
    D. none of the above.

65. Index fossils are often used by geologists to identify the age of rocks. Index fossils are fossils

    A. that are easily recognizable.
    B. that are found over a wide range of territory.
    C. occur in only a few rock layers.
    D. all of the above.

66. A single rock layer that has the same characteristics and usefulness as an index fossil is called a

    A. key bed.
    B. stratified rock layer.
    C. trilobite.
    D. rift bed.

67. Geologists often compare and match rock layers in different areas. These areas must

    A. be very close together.
    B. be on the same continent.
    C. have outcrops.
    D. none of the above.

68. Oil drilling has helped geologists by

    A. unearthing fossil beds.
    B. providing long cores of sedimentary rock for study.
    C. providing samples of microorganisms in the soil for study.
    D. all of the above.

69. Radioactive isotopes found in rocks help geologists determine

    A. what types of organisms lived in an area.
    B. the precise age of a rock.
    C. climatic changes that took place in a given area.
    D. the coarse of evolution in an area.

70. Most geologists believe that the continents of today

    A. were once part of one large landmass.
    B. were always discrete geological areas separated by water.
    C. underwent few changes over time.
    D. formed as a result of meteor impacts.

For 71–80, match the terms in Column A with the descriptions in Column B.

Column A

____ 71. nebulae

____ 72. galaxies

____ 73. nova

____ 74. red giant

____ 75. black hole

____ 76. pulsating stars

____ 77. supernova

____ 78. white dwarf

____ 79. protostar

____ 80. neutron star

Column B

A. a stable star that shrinks and then expands again

B. a collapsed star that can no longer produce energy

C. the explosion of a massive red giant

D. spiral, elliptical, or irregularly shaped clusters, containing millions or billions of stars

E. large clouds of gas and dust found in space

F. areas within a nebula that contract, becoming denser and so hot that they start to glow

G. a brief rebirth of a white dwarf

H. a collapsed star with a core so dense and gravitational field so strong that its own light cannot escape

I. a star with a very dense core that is formed from a supernova

J. a type of star whose brightness varies as it expands and contracts

81. Place the following terms in the order that **best** represents the life cycle of a star.

   white dwarf   neutron star   red giant   protostar   supernova   nebulae

   _____

   _____

   _____

   _____

   _____

   _____

82. The Big Bang Theory maintains that stars and galaxies were formed
   A. about 15 billion years ago.
   B. as a result of an explosion of one dense sphere of hydrogen gas.
   C. from an expanding hydrogen cloud and that the universe is still expanding.
   D. all of the above.

83. If you were traveling through our solar system and your spacecraft landed on a very large planet with a gaseous surface composed mainly of hydrogen and helium, you would most likely be on
   A. Mars.
   B. Venus.
   C. Pluto.
   D. Jupiter.

84. All of the following are names of spacecraft that have explored the solar system **except**
   A. *Viking*.
   B. *Mariner*.
   C. *Villager*.
   D. *Voyager*.

85. If you were traveling through our solar system and found yourself approaching a planet without any natural satellites (moons), you would most likely be
   A. approaching Saturn.
   B. approaching Pluto.
   C. approaching Venus.
   D. incorrect because all planets in our solar system have at least one satellite.

86. If a space probe was destroyed by a collision with an asteroid, what was the most likely position of the probe in our solar system?

   A. between Earth and Mars
   B. between Mars and Jupiter
   C. near the rings of Saturn
   D. anywhere in our solar system

87. A *meteoroid* is a rock fragment traveling in space. Meteoroids enter our atmosphere

   A. whenever Earth's orbit crosses the orbit of a meteor swarm.
   B. during a meteor shower.
   C. fairly regularly.
   D. all of the above.

88. While observing the night sky through a telescope, you observe a glowing object with a long bright tail. It is not visible without your telescope. This object is most likely

   A. an asteroid heading straight toward Earth.
   B. a comet.
   C. a meteor that is part of a meteor shower.
   D. a shooting star.

For questions 89–93, match the term in column A with its best match in column B.

Column A

___ 89. Apollo

___ 90. *Viking*

___ 91. Skylab

___ 92. Hubble

___ 93. Landsat

Column B

A. spacecraft that sent probes to study the surface of Mars

B. a satellite that gathers data used in map-making

C. space missions designed to study the moon

D. an orbiting, manned solar observatory

E. a powerful telescope orbiting above the Earth

94. Scientists observe the surface of the sun safely with the use of

   A. a pair of binoculars.
   B. a solar cell.
   C. a solar telescope.
   D. an optical telescope.

95. Telescopes enable scientists to study

   A. visible light emitted from objects in space.
   B. radio waves and other parts of the electromagnetic spectrum.
   C. both A and B.
   D. none of the above.

96. Like all other stars, the sun's energy is derived from a nuclear fusion reaction at its core. In this reaction, mass is converted to energy when

   A. four hydrogen nuclei join to form a helium nucleus.
   B. two hydrogen nuclei join to form a helium nucleus.
   C. a helium atom splits to form four hydrogen nuclei.
   D. radioactive isotopes of hydrogen decay.

97. The outermost layer of the sun's atmosphere that is only visible during a solar eclipse is the

   A. corona.
   B. photosphere.
   C. chromosphere.
   D. hydrosphere.

98. Electrical disturbances and disturbances in radio and television reception accompany

   A. increased sunspot activity.
   B. solar wind bursts from phenomena, such as solar flares.
   C. tears in the corona called coronal holes.
   D. all of the above.

99. Which of the following is **not** true about the earth-centered, or geocentric, model of the solar system?

   A. Earth is the center of the solar system with the planets revolving around Earth in small circular orbits called epicycles.
   B. Copernicus proposed this model in the 1600s.
   C. Ptolemy proposed this model in about 140 C.E.
   D. Galileo's observations refuted this model.

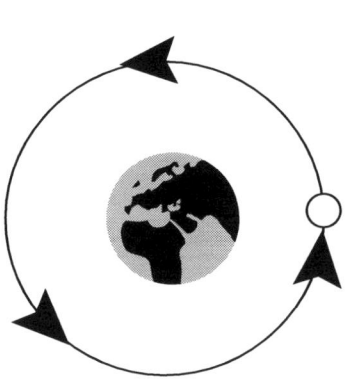
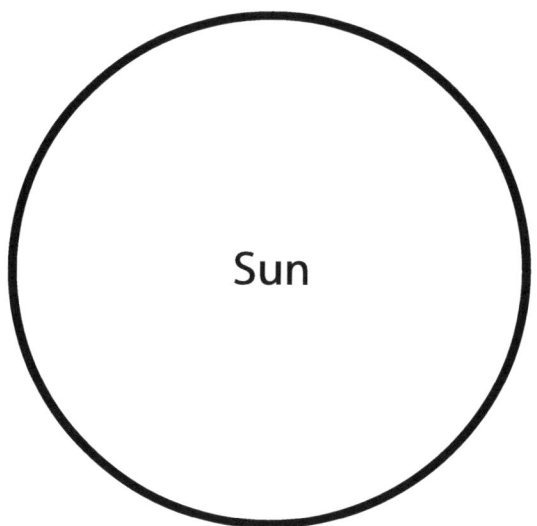

100. Which statement is **not** true about the sun-centered, or heliocentric, model of the solar system?

   A. Ptolemy proposed the model in the 1600s.
   B. The Earth and the other planets revolve around the sun in individual orbits and not in epicycles.
   C. Galileo's observations helped confirm the model.
   D. This model was refined by Kepler's Laws of Planetary Motion.

101. The tides on Earth are caused by the

   A. gravitational pull of the Earth's natural satellite, the moon.
   B. gravitational pulls of the sun.
   C. combined gravitational pulls of both the sun and the moon.
   D. rotation of the Earth alone.

102. The highest tides and lowest tides are called *spring tides*. These tides occur

   A. in areas of Earth that are in direct line with both the moon and the sun.
   B. in areas of the Earth that are in direct line with the moon while the sun is 90 degrees away from the moon.
   C. in areas of the Earth when quarter moons occur.
   D. once in the spring and once in the fall.

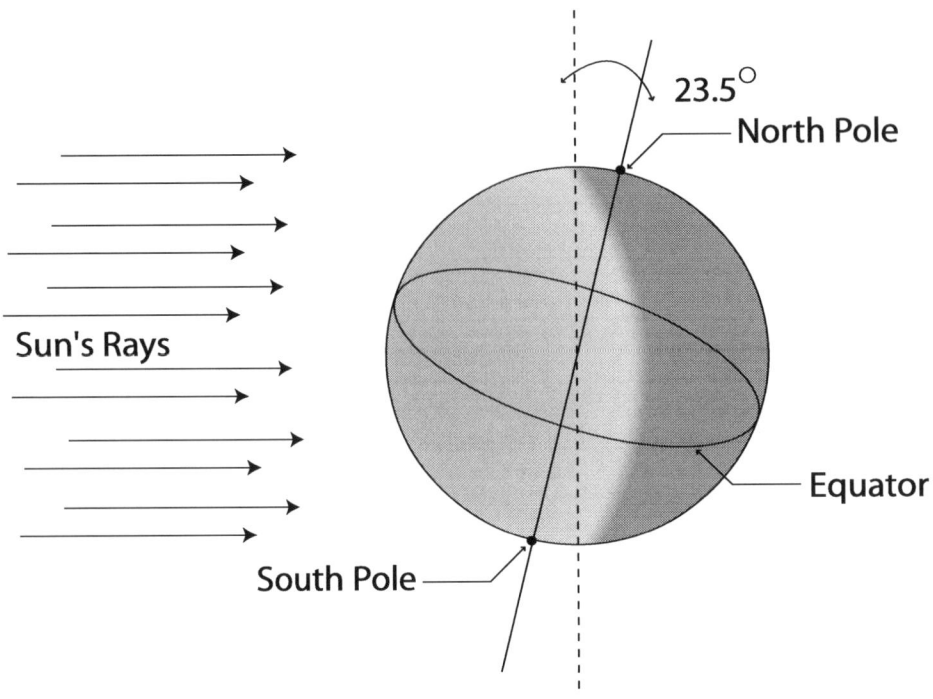

103. Which of the following statements describes the Earth's orbit around the sun?

   A. The Earth revolves around the sun in a circular path.
   B. The Earth orbits around the sun in an elliptical path.
   C. The Earth's distance from the sun is constant throughout its orbit.
   D. The Earth travels around the sun at a constant speed.

104. As the Earth orbits the sun, it rotates on an axis that

   A. has the same tilt throughout the year.
   B. varies in tilt throughout the year.
   C. has no tilt.
   D. none of the above.

105. All of the following are somehow affected by the rotation of the Earth on its axis **except** the

   A. movements of the winds over the Earth's surface.
   B. movements of ocean currents.
   C. intensity of sunlight at various locations on the Earth throughout the year.
   D. rising and setting of the sun.

106. To pinpoint the location of your school on Earth, you need to determine its

   A. latitude.
   B. longitude.
   C. both A and B.
   D. latitude, longitude, and altitude.

107. Latitudes above and below the equator experience seasonal changes in temperature and in the amount of daylight. This is due to

   A. the Earth's axial tilt.
   B. variations in the Earth's distance from the sun during its orbit.
   C. the Earth's axial tilt and its revolution around the sun.
   D. the Earth's rotation and revolution around the sun.

Use this paragraph to answer questions 108–111.

It is late June in New England and your family is host to a foreign exchange student from Brazil named Carlos. Carlos will spend the next year in New England. The day after Carlos arrives, New England experiences its longest period of daylight.

108. On this day,

   A. the Northern Hemisphere is tilted 23.5 degrees toward the sun.
   B. Carlos's homeland is tilted 23.5 degrees away from the sun.
   C. Carlos's friends in Brazil are experiencing Brazil's shortest period of daylight.
   D. all of the above.

109. On this day, the occupants of a weather station very near the North Pole would experience

   A. constant daylight.
   B. constant darkness.
   C. a period of daylight similar to that in New England.
   D. none of the above.

110. Six months from this day, sometime in late December, New England will experience its shortest period of daylight. On this day,

   A. the Northern Hemisphere is tilted 23.5 degrees away from the sun.
   B. Carlos's homeland is tilted 23.5 degrees toward the sun.
   C. the occupants of the weather station in the Arctic Circle will experience constant darkness.
   D. all of the above.

111. Midway between June and December,

    A. the length of the day in New England will be shorter than in Brazil.
    B. the length of the day in Brazil will be shorter than in New England.
    C. the length of the day will be about the same in New England and Brazil.
    D. Not enough information is given.

112. What seasons occur in New England when the Earth's axis of rotation is tipped **toward** and **away** from the sun, respectively?

    A. winter and summer, respectively
    B. summer and spring, respectively
    C. summer and winter, respectively
    D. winter and spring, respectively

113. Where would you live if you wanted little or no seasonal changes in temperature and/or amount of daylight hours throughout the year?

    A. in the Arctic circle
    B. at or near the equator
    C. in the Antarctic Circle
    D. any of the above

1. Describe some of the ways human activities can make water sources harmful to living things.

2. What is eutrophication and how is it a result of human activities?

3. Describe three ways human activity can cause air pollution.

4. Describe three methods of remote sensing that are currently used to generate maps. Describe other ways computer-generated satellite imaging (CGSI) is being used to provide scientists with useful information.

5. What is a rock and how are the three types of rocks formed?

6. Describe how the formation and breakdown of the three main types of rocks are interrelated (the rock cycle).

7. Compare the more traditional model of the composition of the Earth with that of the model of plate tectonics.

8. How is the theory of continental drift related to the theory of plate tectonics?

9. There is a proposal to build a nuclear power plant within a few miles of your community. What are the advantages (benefits) and disadvantages (costs) of having a nuclear power plant so close to home?

10. What is risk-assessment analysis and what are some of the problems associated with its use?

11. Describe some of the reasons people do not support pollution control legislation.

12. Why do earthquakes and volcanoes occur at certain areas of the Earth?

13. Describe some of the causes of mechanical weathering.

14. Describe three processes that result in chemical weathering.

15. Describe how biological factors can aid or result in mechanical or chemical weathering.

16. How do renewable resources differ from nonrenewable resources? Give examples of each.

17. List several ways we can reduce our dependence on fossil fuels.

18. How do we benefit the environment when we reduce, recycle, and reuse?

19. Describe several renewable energy sources and their advantages and disadvantages.

20. What is the difference between an active and a passive solar heating system?

21. How are the levels of oxygen and carbon dioxide in our atmosphere replenished?

22. How can deforestation adversely affect our environment?

23. Describe the advantages and disadvantages of using petroleum products as fuels.

24. Describe some of the problems with the widescale use of synthetic polymers.

25. How does running water create new landforms and break down existing ones?

26. What is the ozone layer and why is it important?

27. What are chlorofluorocarbons and why are they bad for our environment?

28. Describe the structure of the atmosphere with regard to temperature and weather events.

29. What is the ionosphere, how is it formed, and why is it important?

30. Describe three types of severe storms and how they are formed.

31. Describe the characteristics of the ocean floor and how they are related to the theory of plate tectonics.

32. What are glaciers and ice sheets?

33. Describe three instruments astronomers use to study the universe.

34. Your friend Seth is an amateur astronomer. He mentions in class that the universe was formed as a result of a huge explosion billions of years ago and is believed to be expanding. Seth is asked to explain this to the class. What would his explanation be?

35. What evidence led to the formation of the Big Bang Theory of the formation of the universe?

36. One alternative to the Big Bang Theory of the creation of the universe is the Steady State Theory. How does this theory differ from the Big Bang Theory and what lines of evidence argue for or against it?

37. Describe the parts of our solar system and compare the geocentric and heliocentric theories of the solar system.

38. Compare the properties of the planets. Which are most like Earth?

39. What causes the seasons?

The chart below lists the characteristics of the Earth and an imaginary planet Rondo. Use the data in the chart to answer questions 40 and 41.

Characteristics of Earth and Rondo

		Earth	Rondo
Atmospheric Content	Oxygen Levels	21.0%	5.0%
	Carbon Dioxide Levels	0.03%	60.0%
	Nitrogen Levels	78.0%	10.0%
	Levels of Trace Gases	0.97%	25.0%
	Ozone Layer	yes	no
	Distance from a Star	148,640,000 km	100,000,000 km
	Rotation	24 hours	230 days
	Revolution	365 days	230 days
	Diameter	7,930 miles	7,930 miles
	Density	5.50 g/cm^3	2.750 g/cm^3
	Axis Tilt	23.5 degrees	0 degrees

40. Compare conditions on Earth with those on Rondo.

41. Describe three reasons why it would be difficult for life "as we know it" to survive on Rondo.

42. Discuss the pros and cons of the space program.

Made in the USA
Lexington, KY
04 August 2019